CONTENTS

Biddy Baxter and **Edward Barnes** devised and wrote the **Blue Peter Book**

£2.75

Hello

And for the first time ever, Blue Peter viewers have designed the beginning and end of our book!

Two sixteen-year olds, David McCamley of Dublin and Jennifer James of Chorley, were both Top Prize winners in our Intel Post competition. After visiting TV Centre to collect their Awards, by a strange coincidence, David and Jennifer both sent us cartoon drawings as a "thank you" for their day in the Blue Peter studio. By an even stranger coincidence, the thing that obviously made the biggest impression on them wasn't the cameras, or being on the telly, or even us – it was the immense amount of cables that snake their way all over the studio floor, up the walls, and all over the lights in the roof! If you take a close look at their cartoons, you'll see just how many cables they've drawn, and that's what gave us the idea for our competition – so turn to page 77 if you'd like to have a go.

We've packed a great deal into our Silver Jubilee Year, and you'll find some of the highlights in this 21st Book. Most exciting of all is Janet's training for her attempt to

There!

regain the UK Civilian Free Fall record for Blue Peter. So far she's jumped from 12,000 feet. To create a new record, she'll have to leap from 27,500 feet!

After three years on the programme, Peter's off to tackle a new challenge. In his "Duncan Dares . . ." series, he'll be stretching himself to the limits of his strength, endurance and daring, so watch out for news of how he gets on in the reports he'll be sending back to Blue Peter. And don't forget – if you send us a really good idea, as well as being put on the programme, it may well end up in our book – so start thinking, and who knows, this time *next* year, it might be in print!

Simon Groom   Pete Duncan

Janet Ellis

George   Jack   Goldie

3

you recognise any
he photographs?

n to page 76
the answers.

6

7

11

12

Even walking on the net is a special skill.

"My lords, ladies and gentlemen! From South Africa – The Flying Rochelles!"

I felt a shiver of excitement as I sat in the dark and watched Kay, Ian and Joe run out into the ring with their long, silken cloaks shimmering in the spotlight.

The circus has always fascinated me. I suppose it's the mixture of the glamour of show business and the skill and daring of the performers. And nowhere is that more evident than on the Flying Trapeze.

It all looked very different in the cold light of day. There was no spotlight, no drum roll, and no applause. Just three dedicated people in jeans and T-shirts. The only sounds were the sinister creaks of the ropes and the cries of "Pret" and "Hup" – the international circus words that mean "ready" and "go".

The Rochelles are not from a circus family. Joe was bitten by the circus bug when he was at university. He says that flying is the nearest that a human can get to the freedom of the birds. Joe is the "catcher"; his wife, Kay, and Ian are the "flyers".

"You're going a fraction of a second too early – so when you come out of the second somersault, you're hitting my face and not my wrists." Joe was talking to Ian as he sat on his catcher's cradle, swinging 35 metres above the ground. He sounded as though he was chatting over a cup of tea. He looked down and saw me peering up from the floor. He waved and called in a South African accent: "Hello, Pete! Why don't you come up and join us?"

I climbed up the rope ladder to the platform and Joe pulled the trapeze towards me. "Lift the bar up to above head height – and at the same time take your other hand off the back and put it on the bar. Then lift your feet off the platform. Do not leap forward!"

I was glad to feel Joe's reassuring arm encircle my stomach as I took my left arm from the support. I eased up on my toes – and I was away!

"That's it – go with the trapeze – like a pendulum."

It was a wonderful sensation. "Push over – Push over – that's it." After four swings my arms were beginning to pull out of their sockets.

"Let go at the top of the swing. I'll give a 'Hup'. Hup!"

I hit the net and tried to stand before I bounced, which led to several back somersaults and gales of laughter from the platform.

"If you fail as a flyer, we'll book you for a clown!" shouted Joe. All the laughter stopped when I got back to the platform. "Up here you've got to concentrate for every second, Peter, and listen to every word I say."

The next time I took off on my own without Joe's supporting arm – and let go at the same moment as the command "Hup" from the

The narrow platform, 35 metres above the ring, suddenly seemed to be overcrowded.

FLIER

I felt Joe's hands grab my legs – and then let go ...

"Put your other hand on the bar and lift your feet off the platform," Joe said. "Do not leap forward!"

... The next moment I was swinging upside down above the ring.

platform. I was improving.

Joe told me to lie down on the floor of the ring for the next piece of instruction. "This is the position we'll be in for the pass. You will swing towards me – I'll be upside down and I'll grab your legs from behind. You turn your toes *in* – to the hook position."

"When do I let go?" I asked.

"As soon as you feel me grab you."

Kay rolled up the legs of her jeans to give Joe something to grip on and gave me a demonstration. She made a perfect pass, but on her return, a flash of light caused her to lose sight of the bar for a split second and she almost fell.

"See what I mean about concentration," said Joe over his shoulder as he sat on the swinging cradle. "You've only got about a 10th of a second when you turn to sight the bar!" He slipped his legs into the supports and was upside down again, in the catching position. I braced myself ready to swing. "Pret," called Kay when Joe's swing was right for me, but I jerked forward as I left the platform and didn't get an even swing. The next time the rhythm was wrong, which took me too far ahead of Joe's swing.

But the third time I was right. I felt Joe's hands clutch my calves – "Hup" he called – and I let go. The next second I was upside down with rows of wooden seats hurtling towards me like an express train.

"What do I do now?" I yelled.

"Grab a hold of my wrists..."

My stomach muscles needed no second telling! "One more swing – Hup!" – and I was safely down in the net again.

But that was only half of it. I now had to learn to complete the trick and return to the bar. It was then I realised just how difficult it was to spot the moving bar against lights when you're upside down – and turning. I just couldn't get it right, and I made countless trips down to the net and back up to the platform. My arms and legs were killing me – but I wasn't going to give up.

"Don't try to rush it, Pete – look for the platform and the bar will appear in the right place."

I made the pass again – and on the return swing I turned just that little bit earlier – looked for the platform – and there, just as Joe had promised, the gleaming white bar appeared. I felt as though I had all the time in the world as I launched into it and felt the smooth, round rod glide into my palms. It was like

As I turned, the bar appeared out of the darkness – and I launched myself forward.

putting on a glove. Kay and Ian were as excited as I was as they eased me back on the platform.

That was supposed to be that – the wrap, as they call it in the film business. Time to go home and learn next Thursday's script. But Joe had other ideas. He touched my arm as we were preparing to go.

"Pete – how about joining us in the show tonight?"

"You mean in front of an audience?" I asked incredulously.

"Well, I hope so!" He laughed, and Kay and Ian joined in. Kay looked straight at me. "We'd really like you to, Peter." It was an offer I couldn't refuse. I really loved dressing up in the trapeze artiste's gear. I suppose it must be the actor that's still inside me. They fixed me up with a magnificent pair of blue tights, and Mrs Hassani herself, the circus proprietor, lent me a glittering gold belt.

I watched through a chink in the curtain with amazement, admiration and growing terror as Ian completed 2½ somersaults from the bar, his calves landing with a click into Joe's huge hands.

"Ladies and Gentlemen. Tonight the Flying Rochelles have a guest artiste – Peter Duncan of Blue Peter."

I ran out into the spotlight and bowed to the applause. I swung myself up into the net and began the long climb to the platform. Ian and Kay were there to greet me and Joe gave a wink as he sat in the cradle waiting for me to get into the flying position. The drum roll began. I stretched up for the bar and let my feet leave the perch.

I knew I was wrong as soon as I took off.

Thanks to Joe I just made the pass, but I was hopelessly wrong for the return to the bar. I reached up for Joe's wrists, swung back, and dropped ignominiously into the net.

I had failed.

The Ring Master did his best. "Ladies and Gentlemen. Peter Duncan!" he called. And there was some polite applause. I picked myself up from the net and thought: "I'm not going to leave it there." So I pointed up to the platform and began the long climb back. "I'm not going to fail this time," I said to

myself. "Come to think of it – I daren't!"

The drum roll began again. Joe slid down into his catching position. Kay hooked back the trapeze and put it into my hand.

"Don't rush it, Peter – remember how much time you had this morning."

I was off.

The swing was right. I saw Joe looking confident upside down as I hurtled towards him. The pass was right. I felt Joe's hand round my legs and let go... Now the moment of truth. Upside down on the return swing – look for the platform, I told

myself. And there – huge and magnificent – came the gleaming white bar!

Thwack! I was on it and on my way back to Ian and Kay. "Hey!" they called and extended their arms towards me.

"Ladies and Gentlemen – Peter Duncan!" shouted the Ring Master above the deafening applause.

It was, quite simply, the most terrifying moment of my life!

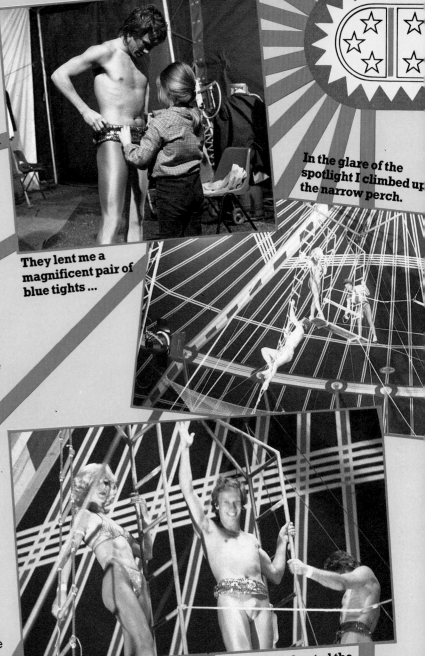

In the glare of the spotlight I climbed up the narrow perch.

They lent me a magnificent pair of blue tights ...

"Ladies and Gentlemen – Mr Peter Duncan!" shouted the Ring Master over the deafening applause.

WeatherBeaters!

Dear Blue Peter,
Do you think that you
could have a Blue Peter
appeal to help the people
that are affected by the
African drought. I heard on
Newsround how bad it all
was and how everybody had so
little food.
Yours sincerly
Julie Pybus age 9

6/10/83

BLUE PETER · **WeatherBeater APPEAL**

FLOODS

DROUGHT

KEY
FLOOD
DROUGHT

. . . world weather crisis . . .
thousands of villages need your help

1983 was a disaster year for tens of millions of the world's poorest people. More than forty countries in Africa, Asia and Latin America suffered the most terrible droughts and floods, and the destruction will take years to repair. The cause? Freak weather conditions – put quite simply – the weather went crazy!

As soon as news of the freak weather conditions began to be reported on the News Bulletins and in the papers, we received hundreds of letters like Julie's. But when we started to delve into the problems caused by the weather, we almost gave up the idea of trying to help. How on earth could we get people in Britain, where the

Our WeatherBeater Telex and News Desk brought us instant reports from all over the world.

Viewers asked us to help the victims of floods and droughts.

Weather Beater
£250,000
£200,000
£175,000
£150,000

9

weather can cause chaos but rarely death – and never mass starvation – to understand the worldwide devastation it had caused? And how could we possibly do anything to help? These are just a few of the desperate problems the weather had caused:

In **Bolivia** more than a quarter of the population – one and a half million people – were desperately short of food because drought had ruined their crops. One town in **Northern Peru,** with an average yearly rainfall of 25 mm had been inundated with 390 cm in 8 months – nearly four times the annual rainfall of England and Wales – and homes, crops, roads and bridges had been destroyed. Yet in **Southern Peru,** high in the Andes mountains, bordering Lake Titicaca, drought had struck. The people had lost three-quarters of their potato crop – their main source of food – and were in danger of starving to death. A coastal town in **Bangladesh** received over 100 cm of rain in three days, and thousands of families were homeless. In **Ethiopia,** where drought and war had destroyed crops, emergency food supplies could not be distributed because roads were non-existent or in bad repair. In **Brazil** and many African countries, families were fighting to survive seriously reduced harvests, and torrential floods brought death and misery to north-west **Nepal.**

What all these countries have in common is that, even when the weather is good, most of the people that live in them are poor. They can only just about survive – even when the weather is kind. Earlier in 1983 there were floods or heatwaves in many parts of Europe and a terrible drought in Australia. But it is the poorer countries where freak weather hits the hardest. **Poor** people are already struggling with many problems like unclean water, bad health, and not enough work or land to buy or grow enough food. The loss of crops or livelihood can be the difference between life or death.

The greatest disaster of all is poverty itself. And that will only be solved when the rich countries of the world make a long-term

Drought-stricken Rajasthan, in Northern India, needed pure water supplies for 16,000 families. A giant tanker, capable of carrying 10,000 litres of water, would be filled from outside the drought area and driven to towns and outlying villages.

For Bolivia we wanted to send 72 tonnes of barley seed and 800 kilos of broad bean seeds to provide crops for 4,000 families in the drought area – and Southern Peru, also suffering from drought, needed 12,000 kilos of potato seed to plant as the staple diet for 1,000 families, plus fertilisers, pesticides and the transport to distribute them.

commitment to help their poor neighbours. But the need for immediate help is desperate, too. Just when we were feeling at our most depressed, another letter arrived, and one sentence in particular made us determined to do something.

"It may only be a small drop in a large ocean, but I feel we must do something to help the starving children."

"Think of what Blue Peter viewers have done in the past," said Simon. "Every little *does* help."

"Cambodia proved that," said Peter, "the results of that Appeal were amazing."

"Was that the first of the Great Blue Peter Bring & Buy Sales?" Janet asked.

"Yes – and it's the best way for fast fund-raising we've ever come across," said Simon. "Let's have a go, then at least some of those families will get help."

We discovered that if our Bring & Buy Sales raised £250,000, we could help 25,000 families pick up the threads of a new life – it worked out at an average of £10 per family.

To our delight, the moment we announced details of our Appeal, there was an instant demand for WeatherBeater Bring & Buy Sale kits. Not only that, the Blue Peter shelves in every Oxfam shop in Britain were full to overflowing. This gave everyone the chance of being either a Bringer or Buyer, and with all the Sales marked on our studio map, and daily reports flowing into our WeatherBeater News Desk, it seemed as though there were WeatherBeaters in every town and village in the land!

Because the crisis had hit poor countries where communications were difficult, it was hard to get film reports of the situations we were trying to help. But we were able to see two of the trouble spots for ourselves and the films we made, left Blue Peter viewers in no doubt that the WeatherBeater Appeal was a matter of life or death.

Simon reported from Peru and discovered it was a freak current of water in the Pacific Ocean that had caused both drought *and* floods. It's called "El Nino" which is Spanish for "the child", meaning the Christ-child, because almost every year, near Christmas, a weak, warm current appears off the coasts of Peru and Ecuador. The 1983 El Nino was different. It extended far out into the Pacific, nearly a quarter of the way around the globe from Peru and Ecuador. It raised the sea level surface off Peru about 5 cm and the tempera-

Part of our WeatherBeater aid provided feeding kits for some of the starving babies – like this one in Somalia.

In flooded Bangladesh we aimed to provide bamboo poles and straw to build houses for 500 families, plus matches, candles, rice, flour, cattle food and seeds to replant crops.

We sent road repairing equipment to the drought area of Ethiopia to enable lorries to deliver emergency food supplies to 750 families in the mountains – 1000 picks, shovels, hoes, plus the running costs for the interim delivery of food supplies in smaller vehicles.

ture of the sea nearly seven degrees above normal. This combined with the trade winds, caused a pile-up of warm water against the land and ended up directly affecting the weather over at least a third of the world – some scientists think even as much as half.

Simon met Oxfam's Field Director for South Peru and Bolivia on the brown and barren shores of Lake Titicaca. Teobaldo Pinzas, or Pocho, as he likes to be called, said that in a normal year, the hills would be green with young crops. The poverty was unbelievable.

Because of the drought, no crops could be grown, so the people were forced to eat their seed potatoes that should have been planted for the following year's crops. Not only were all their livestock dying – there was no food for their children, either. But just before Simon arrived, a little rain had fallen for the first time in two years, and in the village of Unocoya, he saw the first of the Blue Peter seed potatoes being planted.

Simon reported from the village of Unocoya in Southern Peru. He saw the first of the WeatherBeater seed potatoes being planted.

In Bangladesh thousands of villagers like these were homeless. Field Director Saidur Rahman showed Janet where a river had burst its banks.

Five thousand miles away, Janet reported from Govindapur, in Bangladesh, which in four days had received over twenty-five times its normal rainfall! Large areas were still under water, and what were once thriving villages had houses and crops and animals washed away as the rivers burst their banks. Saidur Rahman, the Field Director, said the floods had hit the village Janet visited very early one morning when people were asleep. The village elder, Muzaffar Ali, described how he tried in vain to save his possessions. All he could do was to struggle to an embankment with his wife and children. Three weeks after the flooding, only a few of the families had a roof over their heads.

We know that these reports, together with the telex messages sent to our News Desk, made a great impact on Blue Peter viewers. The proof – just seven weeks after the WeatherBeater Appeal was launched, our second Target of £750,000 was not only reached, but greatly exceeded.

We put all your posters and photos on our WeatherBeater News Desk!

We held our own WeatherBeater Sale in Covent Garden.

On January 2nd, 1984, we were able to announce your Weather-Beater Bring & Buy Sales had raised £1,007,116 and the number of Bring & Buy Sales stood at 14,737.

By mid-May, the figures were £1,610,000 and over 15,000 Bring & Buy Sales. This phenomenal result means that the Weather-Beaters provided aid for 21 of the world's poorest countries. 150,000 families – approximately one million men, women and children have received help, which saved lives and gave them hope for the future.

It has also meant the beginning of new projects designed to make some of the poorest people in the world less vulnerable to freak weather conditions in the future. Thank you, WeatherBeaters!

Thanks to you, we reached our Target in record time!

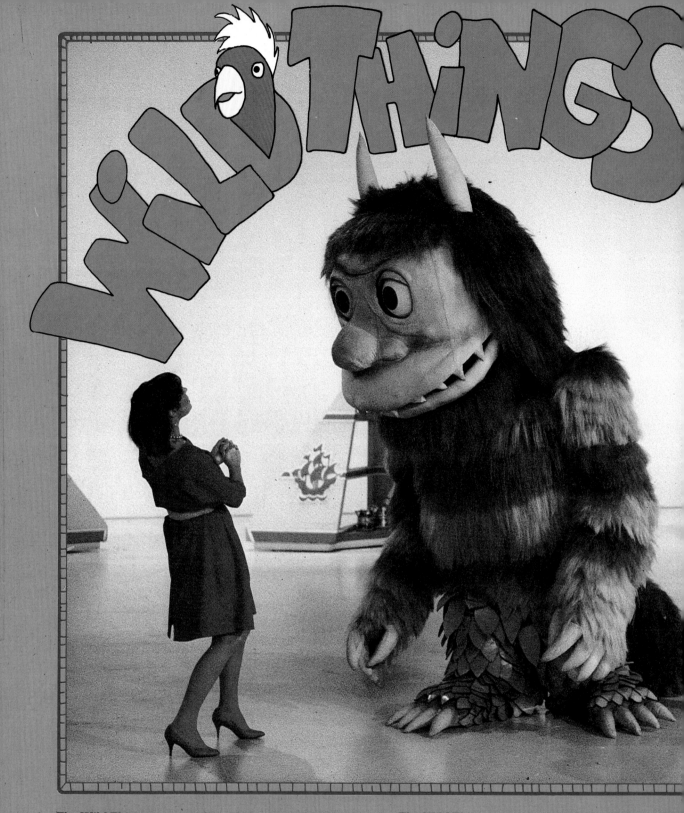

WILD THINGS

The Wild Things came to life in 1984 – complete with radio-controlled eyes – when the composer Oliver Knussen wrote his fantasy opera based on the famous book by Maurice Sendak. The five fantastic costumes took nine months to build. Each one was almost 3 metres tall with gnashing, ferocious teeth and rolling, terrible eyes – and as well as the actors inside the costumes, each Wild Thing had its own radio-control operator, *plus* a singer who spent the entire performance in the orchestra pit!

The Wild Things caused a sensation at the National Theatre, and before their first night, Moishe and Emil caused a sensation at Television Centre when they made their TV debut on Blue Peter. The costumes, weighing a hundredweight each, were so heavy, the actors could only wear them for a few minutes at a time, and the hot studio lights added to the agony. But the final effect was spectacular. As the Wild Rumpus resounded round the studio, the Wild Things reigned supreme at Studio 1, Television Centre!

14

Slipping in to a Wild Thing costume was no easy task! The "skeletons" were massive wire frames, and when they were padded out and covered with yak hair, they weighed a hundredweight each. The actors used levers to operate the giant hands and arms.

Each Wild Thing had its own personal radio-control operator. Caroline Sharman and Vicky Wakley worked the controls for Moishe and Emile's eyes, concealed from the sight of the audience at the side of the stage.

MONSTER MASKS AND CLAWS

17

GO WILD

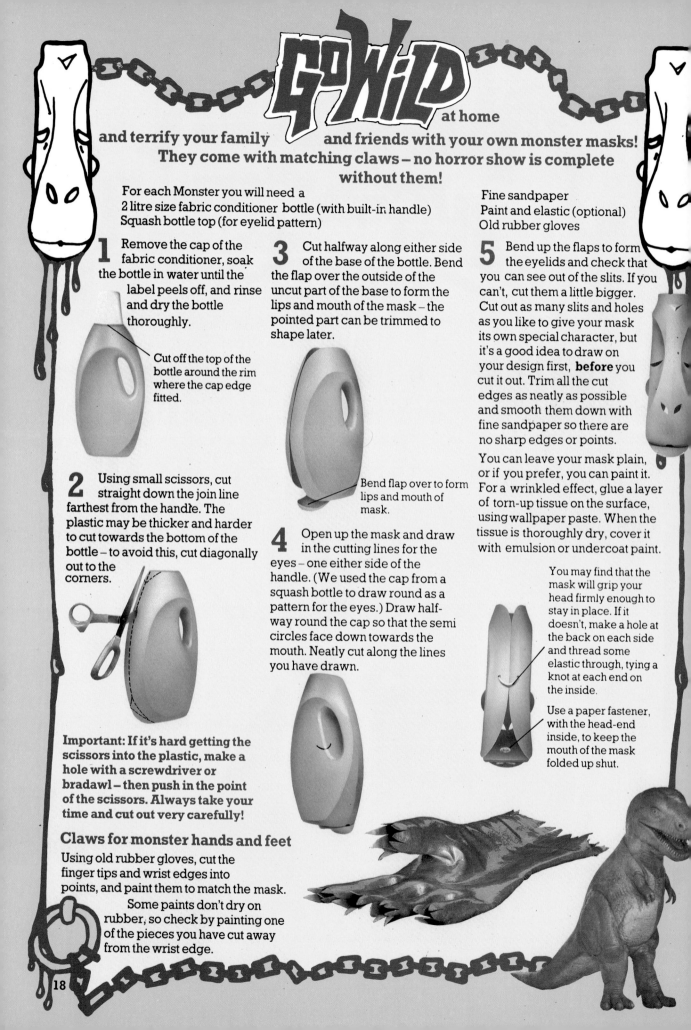

at home and terrify your family and friends with your own monster masks!
They come with matching claws – no horror show is complete without them!

For each Monster you will need a
2 litre size fabric conditioner bottle (with built-in handle)
Squash bottle top (for eyelid pattern)

Fine sandpaper
Paint and elastic (optional)
Old rubber gloves

1 Remove the cap of the fabric conditioner, soak the bottle in water until the label peels off, and rinse and dry the bottle thoroughly.

Cut off the top of the bottle around the rim where the cap edge fitted.

2 Using small scissors, cut straight down the join line farthest from the handle. The plastic may be thicker and harder to cut towards the bottom of the bottle – to avoid this, cut diagonally out to the corners.

Important: If it's hard getting the scissors into the plastic, make a hole with a screwdriver or bradawl – then push in the point of the scissors. Always take your time and cut out very carefully!

Claws for monster hands and feet

Using old rubber gloves, cut the finger tips and wrist edges into points, and paint them to match the mask.

Some paints don't dry on rubber, so check by painting one of the pieces you have cut away from the wrist edge.

3 Cut halfway along either side of the base of the bottle. Bend the flap over the outside of the uncut part of the base to form the lips and mouth of the mask – the pointed part can be trimmed to shape later.

Bend flap over to form lips and mouth of mask.

4 Open up the mask and draw in the cutting lines for the eyes – one either side of the handle. (We used the cap from a squash bottle to draw round as a pattern for the eyes.) Draw halfway round the cap so that the semi circles face down towards the mouth. Neatly cut along the lines you have drawn.

5 Bend up the flaps to form the eyelids and check that you can see out of the slits. If you can't, cut them a little bigger. Cut out as many slits and holes as you like to give your mask its own special character, but it's a good idea to draw on your design first, **before** you cut it out. Trim all the cut edges as neatly as possible and smooth them down with fine sandpaper so there are no sharp edges or points.

You can leave your mask plain, or if you prefer, you can paint it. For a wrinkled effect, glue a layer of torn-up tissue on the surface, using wallpaper paste. When the tissue is thoroughly dry, cover it with emulsion or undercoat paint.

You may find that the mask will grip your head firmly enough to stay in place. If it doesn't, make a hole at the back on each side and thread some elastic through, tying a knot at each end on the inside.

Use a paper fastener, with the head-end inside, to keep the mouth of the mask folded up shut.

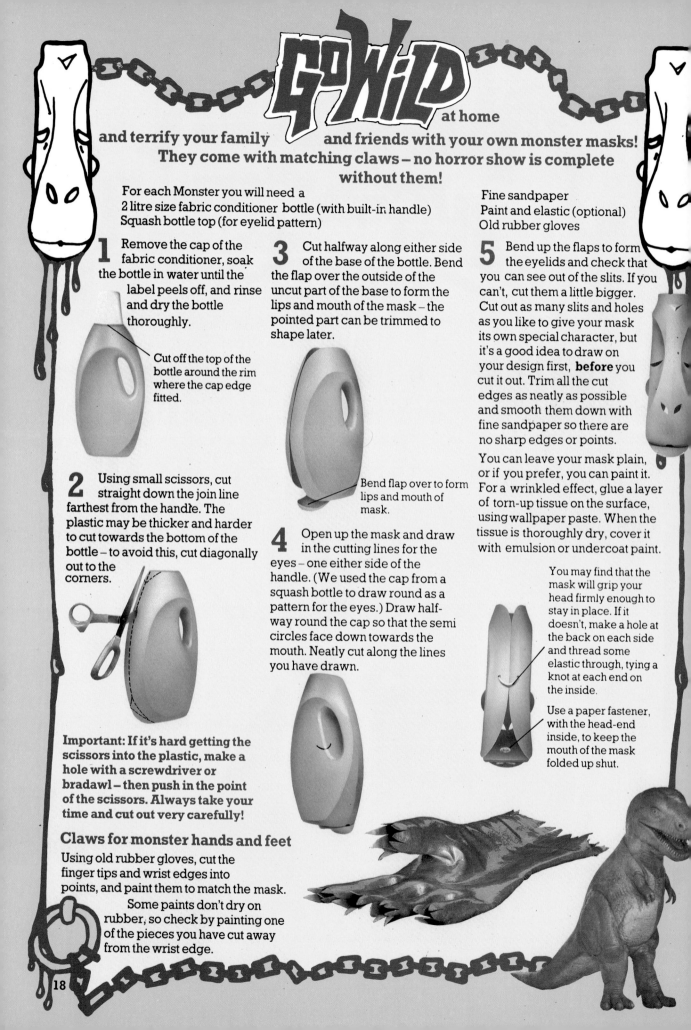

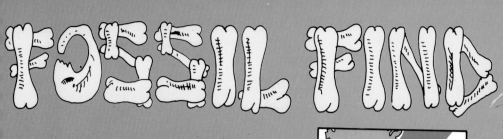

FOSSIL FIND

Imagine Newcastle-upon-Tyne 60 fathoms under the waves, or Sunderland sizzling in temperatures over 50°C. Not so far-fetched as you might think! 240 million years ago, Northumberland *was* covered by the sea, and long before that the whole area was a desert. That's why 13-year-old Sarah Gregory of Blyth made an exciting discovery.

The desert that covered Northumberland and a large chunk of Northern Europe, 240 million years ago.

Dear Simon, Peter and Janet,

I was watching your programme on the 5th Jan. and I was very Intrested in the Fossil Fish which you showed us. I also found a very rare Fossil Fish when I went on a Fossil hunt with the Watch club to a quarry in Durham. We went with a geologist Mr Tim Pettigrew who showed us how to look for Fossils. My dad was showing me how to split an enormous piece of slate and he joked "we go For quantity not quality" but it did have a Fossil in the slate and when I showed it to Mr. Pettigrew he got very excited and told us that it was a Fossil of Wodnika and that it was 240 million years old and that it was the First one to be Found in that area. I wanted to take it home at First but my mam said It "wouldn't Fit the mantlepiece" So I gave it to Tim For the new geology display that was to be opened at Sunderland museum

From
Sarah Gregory 13 years

But that was only the beginning of the story. The detective work was continued by Dr Tim Smithson of Newcastle University. He went to Sarah's quarry and discovered *another* Wodnika! This was a fabulous find – a complete fish curled up and about 45 cm long. (Sarah's would have been much bigger – over a metre in length.) But most exciting of all – only five of these shark-like fish have ever been discovered in Europe. Sarah's Wodnika now has pride of place at the Sunderland Museum – the only exhibit donated by a 13-year-old.

Sarah's Wodnika is only the fifth to have been found in Europe.

Members of the Watch Club searching the quarry at Durham.

The two Wodnikas. Dr Smithson sprayed water on Sarah's to try and make the outline stand out.

The complete Wodnika discovered by Dr Smithson. The shark-like fish had blunt teeth because it used to eat shellfish.

Sarah's fossil – She found the section marked on the sketch which is enlarged in the top photograph. The fish's head is still embedded in the slate – most of the cartilage has disappeared, so the outline is faint.

Wet and watery! An artist's impression of the North-East of England 240 million years ago when the land was 60 fathoms under the sea.

ASTHENOCORMUS!

The fossil fish that inspired Sarah's letter to Blue Peter was even rarer than the Wodnika. It was spotted by Dave Martill, of Leicester University, when he was examining clay pits at Peterborough

Head x-ray

belonging to the London Brick Company.

"I saw a fraction of bone in the clay just below the surface," said Dave. "When we finished digging it out, it measured 2.15 metres from its jaws to its tail!" But this was no common or garden fossil. Experts at the Natural History Museum who identified the bones, said they belonged to an Asthenocormus – another shark-like fish that swam around with marine reptiles 150 million years ago Dave brought the bones to Blue Peter the day before

The Asthenocormus' tail. The 10p piece gives a good idea of its size.

These photographs of two of the German Asthenocormus were taken in 1881.

they were identified as the first Asthenocormus ever to be found in Britain. Only three others have been discovered in the whole of the world and they all came from Germany. Of those, one was destroyed during the Second World War, there's one in America, and the third is still in Germany – so Dave's discovery is not only a first for Britain, it's of enormous, world-wide, scientific importance.

Whenever there's an exciting fossil find, people say "it could never happen to me." But it happened to Sarah and to Dave, so who knows – next time it might be you!

Only a handful of people have ever seen an Asthenocormus – let alone touch one – so we were very lucky indeed to have an Asthenocormus in the studio. And thanks to TV, eight million Blue Peter viewers can now say they've seen one of the world's rarest fossil fish!

Sri Lanka

To visit somewhere you have heard a lot about is a strange experience. It can be a terrible disappointment, because other people's descriptions, photographs and films, can create an impression that the place can't quite live up to.

That was our greatest worry, as we fastened our seat belts for landing at Colombo, the capital of Sri Lanka, because the first Blue Peter team that visited the Island (then called Ceylon) in 1969 have never stopped raving about it.

There's no doubt who stole the show during our Summer Expedition to Sri Lanka – the Elephants!

I was "adopted" by Karmani, a four-month old orphan.

"It's just the best place on earth," Valerie Singleton told us.

Let's just say that Valerie was absolutely right, and leave it at that. Once you've visited Sri Lanka you can't get it out of your mind. We have endless arguments in the dressing room about what we liked best, but for Simon there is no doubt at all. It was the Elephants.

The Elephant is the most useful piece of farm equipment in Sri Lanka. It has great advantages over the tractor. For instance, you don't need an import licence, nor do you need to carry any spares. An elephant has no use for petrol or oil, he's very unlikely to break down, and he can get to places where no wheeled vehicle can penetrate. But his greatest advantage over a machine is his intelligence.

We watched, Abdullah a large bull elephant, knocking down a dead palm-tree in a coconut plantation. The mahout, perched just behind his ears, talked to him all the time in Elephant language. Our guide said the words they used didn't mean anything in any recognisable human tongue. "Akachic. Akachic. Hiro, Hiro. Akachic."

The mahout gave Abdullah a slight thump behind his ear with his bare knee. This brought him head on

Two more babies very obligingly held our clapper board when we filmed at the Elephants' Orphanage.

to the dead tree. He lifted his trunk, wrapped it round the palm-tree, gave it a good shake, and then stepped back again. The elephant was working out just how firmly the tree was embedded in the ground.

Another "Akachic" and a prod behind the ear from the mahout brought Abdullah up to the tree again. This time he put his short tusks either side of the stem, lifted his left foot and put it against the base. Abdullah's enormous back legs dug into the ground and straightened out as he thrust the whole of his massive 4 tons against the tree. There was a pause, and a great "Hhh!" as Abdullah's scaly skin rubbed against the coarse trunk of the palm-tree. He stepped back, paused, and then came at it again with a determined look in his small, beady eyes. You could see every muscle in his enormous body straining as he pushed harder and harder. Then a crack like a pistol shot shattered the silence of the plantation, followed by a groaning sigh and a crash as the 25-metre palm-tree hit the ground.

In 1900 there were 20,000 elephants in Sri Lanka, and today there are scarcely 2,000. The wild elephants in the Jungle are carefully protected, and as a good working elephant is worth up to £12,000, every effort is made to increase the birth rate, and to look after the baby elephants. They even have an Elephant Orphanage, to take care of calves which have been abandoned or lost.

It was there I met Karmani who became my greatest friend in Sri Lanka. Karmani was a 4-month-old bull. He was about a metre tall, and for some reason which I couldn't fathom, he took to me from the moment I arrived. He had been found abandoned in a waterhole in the jungle, and he would certainly have died if the Orphanage hadn't taken him in. Karmani had been selected to be with me when I spoke to camera about the work of the orphanage. As soon as I knelt down beside him, he reared up on

The elephants need a daily bath because their skin gets very cracked and dry in the hot climate.

70-year old Rajah, the greatest of all the elephants, who leads the Perehera at Kandy, has arthritis in his front right knee. I helped to apply a hot, herbal poultice.

High statues of the Lord Buddha have been put up all over Asia. This one is over 1,000 years old.

The Reverend Wimela, who is 10-years old, has ordinary lessons just like any other schoolboy in Sri Lanka.

The monks' training begins at 5 o'clock each morning with two hours' meditation beneath the sacred Bo tree.

his hind legs and tried to climb into my lap like an enormous puppy. Being used to weaned calves on the farm at home, I automatically stuck my thumb in his mouth, and he almost swallowed me whole! A baby elephant will normally drink its mother's milk for the first three years of its life, but Karmani was being bottle-fed – to the extent of 10 litres per day!

The elephants of Sri Lanka have a very strong trade union. They work from 5.00 am until lunch time, and as soon as one o'clock strikes, it's bath-time. In fact, it is illegal to work an elephant for more than six hours a day – but law or no law, when a 4-ton elephant decides to down tools, it would take a brave man to stop him.

The orphanage elephants observe the bathing regulations like their working cousins, and, of course, the elephants in the wild. They need a daily bath because their skins get cracked and dry in hot climates, but apart from that, it's obviously the high spot of their day!

Karmani didn't need a swimming lesson. He followed the big elephants straight into the river and flopped over on his side. I was amazed at the instinctive way he used his trunk as a snorkel, with just a little pink tip appearing above the brown waters of the river.

We got stuck into scrubbing the Elephants with coconut husks and for a while I forgot about Karmani. But he didn't forget me! Every so often I would feel something rasping against my calves beneath the water, and there, sure enough, was Karmani, just checking that I was still there! I wonder if he still remembers me – they say they never forget!

I had the honour of being presented to the most famous elephant in Sri Lanka – the great Rajah, star of the Perehera, the magnificent elephant procession held every year in Kandy. He was also a link with the past on Blue Peter, because he had featured in a film with Val, John and Pete back in 1969. It was Rajah who clouted the Blue Peter film director with a piece of bamboo, because he (Rajah) thought the filming had gone on for long enough! The film director, who is now Head of Children's Programmes, visited Sri Lanka 12 years later on holiday, and Rajah hit him again, just to let him know that he hadn't forgotten!

Rajah is 70 years old now, and although a little arthritic, is still magnificent with his great, gleaming tusks, and very conscious of his position as King of the Elephants. Thikeribunda, the 10-year-old assistant mahout made a herb poultice for Rajah's arthritic knee. No trouble or expense is spared to make sure that Rajah will be fit for the Perehera.

Every August full moon, clad in the most magnificent jewelled caparison, he leads 150 other elephants in the greatest procession in the world. His tusks, are sheathed in gold, and on his back is a golden casket containing the most precious relic in all Sri Lanka – the eye tooth of the Lord Buddha.

The Lord Buddha teaches that long hair leads to vanity, so every three months the boys' heads are completely shaved.

From all over the Island the people come to watch and worship at this great festival because more than half the population of Sri Lanka follow the teachings of the Lord Buddha. Peter had studied Buddhism long before he came to Blue Peter, and he was especially keen to discover more about it.

Buddha was once a Prince who lived in India. He was brought up in the lap of luxury surrounded by immense wealth. But he felt there was something more to life than just being able to clap your hands for a servant to bring everything you wanted, while there was still so much suffering in the world.

So he left his palace, and for six years he wandered all over India, searching for the truth. In the end, exhausted, he sat down under a Bo tree, just as he is sitting in the statue.

All through the night he struggled with the powers of evil. At last, in deep meditation, the truth came to the young Prince, and ever after that he was called the Buddha – the enlightened one, the one who knows.

He knew he must give up everything he owned and travel about teaching everyone to stop being greedy and selfish. He must teach them to strive only for the pure and the good things, never to kill or steal, to help other people, and so find truth and peace.

The faith spread across India, and in 236 BC, Buddhism came to Ceylon.

A branch of the same Bo tree, beneath which Buddha had first learned the truth, was carried to Ceylon and planted. It grew as a symbol that the faith had come to the Island to stay, and today, nearly 2300 years later, that same tree still flourishes and is visited by pilgrims from all over the world.

Saplings from the sacred Bo tree have been planted by every temple in Ceylon, so that a living link with the Lord Buddha will always be there for everyone to see.

Huge statues of the Lord Buddha have been put up all over Asia. We visited some that are over 1000 years old in the ancient ruined city of Pollunarua in the heart of the jungle.

There are no "services" as we know them in the Buddhist religion. But every day at set times in the morning and evening the pipes and the drums signal the faithful to bring their offerings to the temple, and pray before the statue of the Buddha. The Lord Buddha sent monks all over Asia to spread his message of peace, and Buddhist monks with their shaven heads and saffron robes are a common sight in the East today. They have a long training which can start as early as their seventh birthday.

The Reverend Wimela is just ten and he's been a monk for almost a year. His day begins at 5 o'clock in the morning with two hours' meditation beneath the Bo tree.

Wimela has ordinary lessons like any other schoolboy in Sri Lanka – he learns arithmetic, English and his own language, Singhalese. But he also has special lessons, like Pali, which is an ancient Indian language that's no longer spoken. All monks must learn it because most of Buddha's teaching is written in Pali.

Buddha teaches that long hair leads to vanity, so that if a monk has no hair at all, he can stop thinking about himself and concentrate on thinking about others.

Wimela's hair was not exactly long when we arrived. In fact, he looked rather like a skinhead. But this is long by Buddhist standards, so it was off to the monastery barber. It is quite a shock watching a

The first-and-last-time Janet will ever wear £250,000-worth of jewels! They are all mined in Ratnapura where for centuries workers have toiled, up to their waists in water, in deep, dark, smelly pits, to discover sapphires, moonstones and amethysts.

Plucking tea is also a back-breaking job – the Tamil girls work for ten hours a day, often in the blazing sun.

Each basket is carefully weighed because the girls are only paid for what they pick. The wages seem pitiful by Western standards – an average of £5.00 a week.

The drink is called toddy. I tried a glass of it when I was safely back on the ground, and it tasted like yesterday's washing-up water!

Balancing precariously along this thin rope walk-way, 30 metres above the ground, was a very hairy moment. I was following the toddy tapper. He dices with death in the tree tops to tap the juice of the coconut flower which supplies Sri Lanka with a powerful alcoholic drink.

ten-year-old boy having his head completely shaved – but in Sri Lanka it's no more unusual than wearing a school cap is here.

Discipline is strict in the monastery and the boys have a hard and rigorous timetable. It is difficult for anyone living in the West to believe that you could leave a bunch of boys, aged from 5 to 12, to meditate without moving or speaking for two hours!

But after meditation's over, and it's bath time, the boys don't look quite so holy. They stand in twos in front of the well, wearing their under-robes. There are buckets on long ropes because the water level is about 10 metres from the top of the well. The boys fling the buckets down the well with their right hand, and as soon as they're full, a sudden jerk on the rope with the other hand brings the bucket rocketing to the top. In one clean movement it's caught in the right hand, emptied over their heads and flung back down the well again. To do it in "one" was obviously a great point of honour.

But the most important part of Wimela's day are his visits to the temple. Twice every day he takes his offering of lotus flowers and kneels before the statue of the Lord Buddha.

In ten years' time when Wimela is 20, he will be ordained and admitted into the order. He will touch with a staff the seven gifts that are offered to him: a razor, three robes, a needle and cotton, a water filter and a begging bowl. He will own nothing else. His job will be to meditate on the mysteries of the Lord Buddha, and to preach the word of the man who found truth and peace as he sat beneath a Bo tree, 2300 years ago.

Most of the people in Sri Lanka work on the land which is rich and verdant. The climate is so good that you don't need many clothes, the sea is full of fish, and, they say, if you push a stick into the ground it will bear fruit. It sounds wonderful, but the truth is that many of the people are poor and they need to work very hard just to scrape a living.

Valerie was right. It is the most wonderful place on earth. But Sri Lanka is a sadly divided nation. The troubles between the Tamils and the Singhalese, both citizens of Sri Lanka but people of different races and religions, are never far from the surface, and they erupted into violence just after we finished filming.

We look back with pleasure and sadness on our Expedition to Sri Lanka, and our hearts go out to the people, both Tamil and Singhalese, in the hope that they might live together in peace on that most beautiful island.

Half a million bricks went to make the twenty-four arches of Ribblehead Viaduct, striding across the Ribble Valley, carrying the track thirty metres above the ground.

The long drag is the name drivers of steam locomotives used to call the hard pull up to the highest railway station in England, which is one of the great railway journeys of the world.

I have had some memorable train journeys on Blue Peter – through the Rockies on the mighty *Royal Hudson*, and shovelling coal on the footplate of our own steam loco Blue Peter 532, so I jumped at the chance of travelling on the Settle to Carlisle line.

I knew it was one of the most amazing lines in the world, but it never needed to be built at all. In the Railway Age, dozens of separate companies divided the country between them, and there were two routes to Scotland along the East and the West coasts of England. Yet passengers on the Midland Railway had to wait and change trains, because they had no through route.

I waited with Goldie on Settle station for the 10.03 to Carlisle.

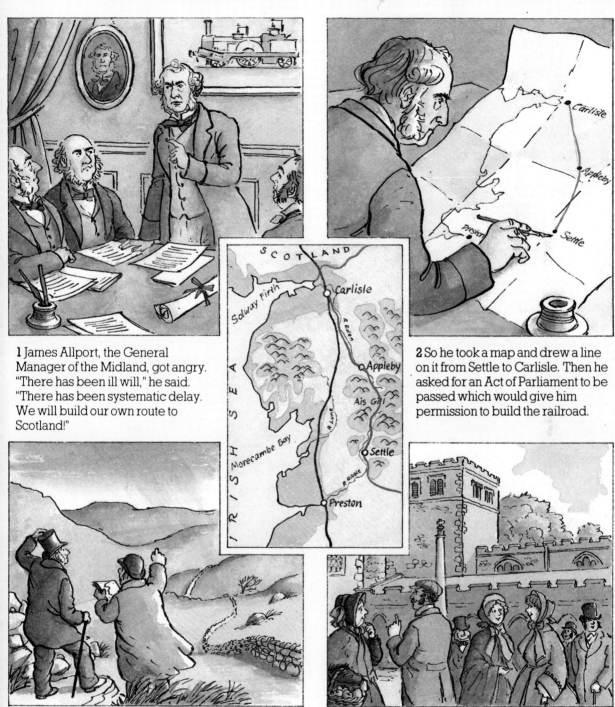

1 James Allport, the General Manager of the Midland, got angry. "There has been ill will," he said. "There has been systematic delay. We will build our own route to Scotland!"

2 So he took a map and drew a line on it from Settle to Carlisle. Then he asked for an Act of Parliament to be passed which would give him permission to build the railroad.

3 But Allport and his Chief Engineer were appalled when they saw the terrain. The line was to be seventy-two miles long across some of the steepest and most impenetrable moorlands in England. There was an average rainfall of 180 cm a year – and the wind howled ceaselessly.

4 When the people of Appleby heard they were going to get their very own line, they rang the church bells joyfully, for their town was going to be put on the map at last, but it wasn't much fun for the railway navvies who had to build the line.

5 There were six thousand men employed building the line – navvies, stone masons, carpenters, clerks and engineers. Pay was good, but hours were long.

6 They dug out Blea Moor tunnel – the highest tunnel in the country, and a mile and a half long. They worked with naked candles, and used dynamite for clearing the ground ahead.

7 They built rough shanties along the track, and plodded back to them after work.

8 These grew into settlements with names like Batty Green, Jerusalem, Belgravia – "Human dwellings have sprung up like mushrooms," it was said.

9 In winter when the wind blew and the snow piled up, the shanty towns must have been very bleak. Many of the workers were killed in accidents, and wives and children became ill and did not recover.

At last it was finished. It had taken six and a half years and cost £3,500,000. There were seventeen viaducts, twelve tunnels and countless embankments and cuttings.

It was a hard journey for the locomotive drivers and their firemen. Settle is 130 metres above sea level, and after that the track keeps climbing for 25 miles, with an overall gradient of one in a hundred. In the days of steam, the locos in their smart green liveries toiled up, consuming huge quantities of coal and water. No wonder they called it The Long Drag.

The top of the Long Drag is Ais Gill, 360 metres above sea level, and the highest point of any main-line railway in England. Nearby Dent station was the highest in England once, but it was closed down a few years ago.

And that is a sad sign of the times.

Only two daily passenger trains in each direction travel between Settle and Carlisle, and Appleby Station – where the trains used to stop for coal and water, and where nine men were employed – is almost deserted.

Even the spectacular Ribblehead Viaduct is showing signs of wear, with great cracks appearing, but British Rail say repairs will be too costly, and threaten to close it down altogether. That would be a great shame, because this stunning achievement of the Railway Age ought to be saved, not only as a priceless part of our country's past, but as a memorial to the men whose brilliance and whose sweated labour have given us one of the most sensational railway journeys of all time.

THE TWO SHAKEYS!

When ten-year-old Marc Jones from Port Talbot, in Wales, came face to face with Shakin' Stevens in the Blue Peter studio, he achieved a lifetime's ambition. Marc had already won 8 cups and medals for his impersonation of Shakey, but he never dreamed that he'd end up in front of TV cameras, broadcasting "live" to eight million viewers. Even Goldie joined in the bopping as the two Shakeys performed *Cry Just a Little Bit* as it had never been seen before!

PUTTING A SPOKE IN IT

There's a long tradition of pulling Groom's leg on Blue Peter. I don't know quite how it began, but there's always someone having me on, hoping that I'll fall for it, and they are not usually disappointed!

So when Alex Leger, who is the Blue Peter filming boss, told me that my next assignment was "Bicycle Polo", my immediate reaction was – try pulling the other one.

I still had lingering doubts when I approached the Purley Way playing fields in South London on a wet and windy Sunday morning. But there, to my surprise, and Goldie's immediate fascination, were the Solent Wheelers, in mid-chukker, against the Chelsea Pedlars.

Bicycle Polo, I later discovered, is a serious game with proper rules. In fact, it is serious enough to have been invented twice, which is more than the horsey version can claim. It took an Irishman to think of it first. Back in 1891, Richard Mecredi, a racing cyclist just past

Goldie and I posed for a pre-match picture with some of the gallant lads from the Solent Wheelers and the Chelsea Pedlars.

his peak, was searching for another way of staying in sport on two wheels. He was so successful that the game became an Olympic sport, and in 1908 an Irish team beat England in the Games held at White City – not a mallet stroke from the Blue Peter studios. Then sadly, Bicycle Polo faded away in the shadow of the first World War, and not a chukker was played for over ten years.

But no one told Cyril Scott. In 1930, he, too, found himself too old for racing, so he invented Bicycle Polo for the second time. Great minds really do think alike when they're confronted by the same problem, because Cyril had never heard of the triumphs of 1908.

32

There are six players on either side, but only five are allowed on the ground at the same time. The sixth can be substituted between chukkers, and there are six 15-minute chukkers to each game. Ron Beckett, an international coach, told me some of the finer points of the game whilst I put on my knee pads, my shin pads and my helmet.

"Some of the lads don't bother with these," he said, and then added ominously, "but mark my words, it's a pretty rough game!"

That is an understatement. Out of the corner of my eye I watched Tony Knight of the Solent Wheelers shoulder charge Nick Mayhew-Sanders of the Chelsea Pedlars at 20 mph, sending him flying over the touch line.

The bicycles are specially adapted with straight forks and tiny handlebars for maximum manoeuvrability. They have no brakes, but fixed wheels, which, with reverse pedalling, will slow you down, but might also shove you over the handlebars.

I tied Goldie to a goal post and took my place for what was described as a friendly chukker.

The game is started by two players belting towards the ball, which is placed in the middle of the pitch. I found I could get up to a fair speed quite quickly. I had my eye on the ball and my mallet raised to strike, just like Prince Charles at Windsor Great Park.

But Tony Knight was right behind me and gaining fast. His shoulder hit mine, and in one flowing movement he belted the ball across his front wheel to a waiting player and sent me hurtling into the mud.

It is not a sport for the faint-hearted. I now discovered in practice that if only I could get on to the ball with my mallet held sideways, I could push it for quite a distance along the ground. In fact, I could, with hard work and dedication, play this game quite well – if it wasn't for the five players on the other side! It is a game of immense skill and judgement, requiring a great deal of courage, and an enormous pair of thigh muscles. My handlebars were at right angles and my saddle was facing backwards after one spirited crash, but a few bangs and bends made me mobile and back into the fray once more. By now it was pouring with rain and the ground was getting softer by the minute, and with our wheels sinking inches into the mud, the effort of pedalling became harder and harder, and I could hardly see through the mud that was splattered all over my face.

At noon the final whistle blew and I crawled back to the touchline and gratefully pulled a sweater over my head. The thought of a hot bath had never seemed so attractive. Through the pain of my aching thighs and the haze of driving rain and mud I asked Tony why he was so keen on Bicycle Polo.

"I play this game because it is great!" he said, simply.

Footnote: At the time of writing, I hear that the Chelsea Pedlars are booked for a tour of India. They are to play at Bombay, Jaipur and Delhi. As *The Times* put it – "A great step forward for a great game."

Great Snakes!

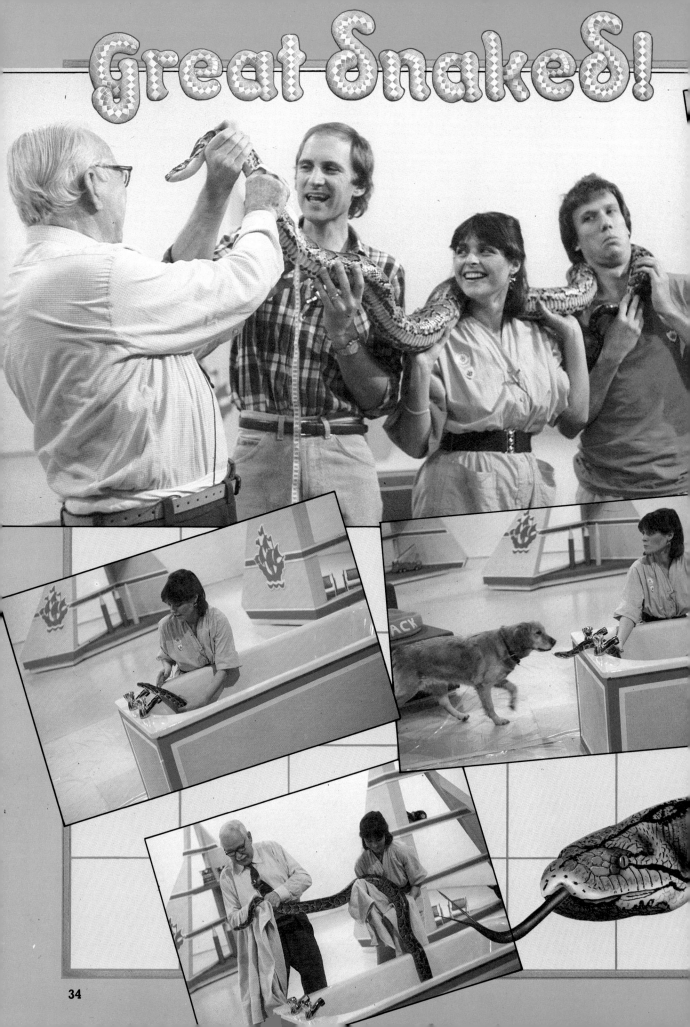

Never in our wildest dreams did we ever think we'd end up bathing a python! And if *you've* ever tried to lift 2½ metres of dripping-wet snake, you'll appreciate our problems. Peter, a five-year-old Rock Python, belongs to the Mace family of Sheffield. They say he enjoys his bath, and George Cansdale told us that in the wild he'd probably spend hours every day submerged in a pool with just his nostrils and eyes above the surface, waiting to pounce on rats and even porcupines.

It took the three of us, plus George, all our time to grapple with Peter – and he's only a baby. When he's fully grown and over 10 metres long – we'll leave bathing him to Mr Mace!

You'd think this was Iceland – not deepest Derbyshire! But early this year, after one of the heaviest snowfalls in living memory, Simon's parents' farm at Dethick looked like the Arctic – with sheep and cows instead of polar bears! Luckily, this new-born lamb survived the great freeze.

My first visit to Dethick got off to a chilly start. But whatever the weather, the animals have to come first, so we loaded up the tractor with bales of hay and set off, with Goldie and her daughter, Lady, leaping after us. Like all dogs, they love the snow, but the 200 sheep were having a pretty tough time. We had to push the tractor out of drifts four times before we fed them – after that, a day in the Blue Peter studio seemed a push-over.

BLUE PETER SLEDGE

Materials

2 pieces   1050 mm × 150 mm × 25mm
Softwood planed all round for the runners

2 pieces   600 mm × 50 mm × 25mm
Softwood planed all round for bracing runners

1 piece   450 mm × 50 mm × 25mm
Softwood planed all round for the footrest

4 pieces   450 mm × 100 mm × 25mm
Softwood planed all round for the seat

30 countersunk woodscrews   38 mm × No. 8

10 countersunk woodscrews   25 mm × No. 8

2 lengths 3 mm × 19 mm aluminium strip 1125 mm long

Waterproof white wood   working glue

Method

1 Clamp the two pieces of 1050 mm × 150 mm wood together and mark off the curve for the front of the runners. Cut out roughly with a saw and finish the curve with a plane or rasp.

2 Take the two lengths of 600 mm × 50 mm and screw and glue them to the inside of the runners, flush with the top and level with the end.

3 Fit the foot-rest; glue and screw it into position.

4 Drill and countersink the sections of 450 × 100 mm. Screw and glue them into position along the top of the runners, starting from the back of the sledge.

5 Drill and countersink the aluminium strip and fit to the bottom of the runners, making sure that the screws are flush with the runners, otherwise they slow the sledge down.

Finally fit a piece of rope to the foot-rest, and your sledge is ready for use. If you have time, it's well worthwhile giving it a coat of paint. This will stop the wood absorbing too much water, and warping, and will keep your sledge in good condition for many years of sledging!

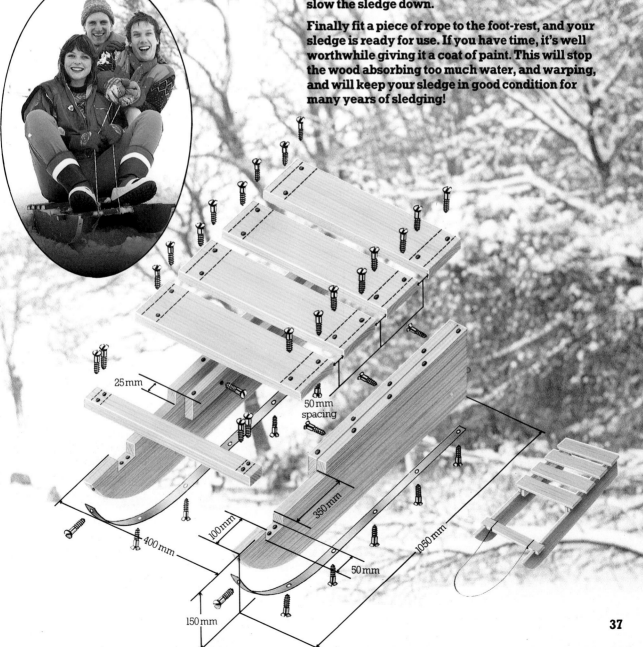

25 mm

50 mm spacing

350 mm

400 mm

100 mm

1050 mm

50 mm

150 mm

'Ear 'Ear

A cheap and cheerful way to cheat the wintery weather!

1 Wind chunky wool over a piece of thick card – don't overlap the strands.

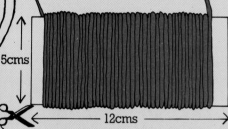

5cms

12cms

Cut through the strands down one side of the card.

2 Measure a strand of wool 60cm long and knot one end.

3 Take a length of the wool cut from the card and fold it in half so that it forms a loop. (If you're using thin wool use more than one strand at a time).

Slip the loop under the long piece of wool and bring the ends over it and down through the loop.

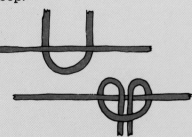

Pull the ends tightly and push the strand down the length of wool to the knotted end.

4 Continue to tie on strands of wool, bunching them tightly together, for just over half the length of wool.

Tie a knot in the long length of wool to hold the strands secure, and cut off the spare wool.

5 Using matching thread, sew the length of knotted strands into a flat, round shape. Starting at one end of the knotted strand, turn it into a tiny circle, securing the shape with fairly large stitches.

Continue spiralling the knotted edge round, and stitching it in position, until the whole length is sewn into a round shape. Keep all the wool strands facing away from the stitching. Firmly oversew the stitches at the end of the spiral.

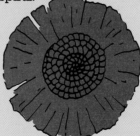

6 Make a second ear-muff in the same way and trim with scissors. Tug the muffs slightly at the ends to give them an oval shape. You can use a teazle or suede brush to fluff up the wool.

7 Cut twelve strands of wool long enough to reach across the top of your head to the middle of your ears. Tie together at one end and plait loosely in three groups of four strands.

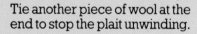

Tie another piece of wool at the end to stop the plait unwinding.

8 Pin the ends of the plait to the inside of each ear-muff, checking they fit across your head and over your ears properly, then oversew the plait firmly in position.

To hold your ear-muffs in place, thread some thin elastic through the bottom edge, and adjust the length so that the muffs fit close to your ears. Tie the ends of the elastic firmly.

P.S. To keep both ears warm, you only need 40g of wool.

THE CASE OF THE TWITCHER'S TELESCOPE

Can you solve this case?
Six careless mistakes gave away the crook.
We spotted them. Can you?

"Harrier!" said Bob.

The former Police Superintendent McCann, nowadays working as a globe-trotting private detective, instantly clapped a pair of powerful binoculars to his eyes. "Got it, Bob," he said.

The great bird glided low over the reed beds, its wings angled slightly upwards to form a shallow vee as it scanned the ground on the hunt for small birds and animals, its clawed legs trailing beneath it. "What is it, Bob?" McCann asked.

"Marsh harrier," Bob replied. "A female – you can tell by the creamy head and chocolate-coloured body." McCann was taking a break from his hectic round-the-world schedule of solving major crimes, and was accompanying his nephew, Bob, on a bird-watching expedition. Both were keen bird-watchers, in a quiet sort of way, and often, when McCann could manage to take a day off from crime-busting in exotic parts of the world, he and Bob would spend an easy day in one of England's many good bird-watching places.

"I must say," said McCann, lowering his binoculars as the harrier glided out of sight, "Great Eddington is an absolutely splendid bird reserve – worth every penny of the one-pound entrance fee. Why haven't we been here before?"

It was Bob who usually planned their expeditions. "It's only just opened," he explained. "It's been on the cards for a long time, but a lot of people were against it. They thought that leaving all this land with its reeds and marshes just for birds, was all wrong. There was a scheme to burn off all the reeds, dig it out, and make a lake for water sports. But the reserve opened this summer, and it has been a great success. Warden's a splendid chap – he's very absent-minded, I know, but terrific at his job."

"I'm glad the birds have got the place," commented McCann. "But a fire would be a disaster here – there hasn't been much rain for ages."

The pair were tramping back to the warden's hut at the entrance to the reserve, both anxious to compare what they had seen with a list of sightings from the previous day. As they turned towards the hut, they met a group of three or four young men walking in the opposite direction. All of them wore anoraks and woolly hats, all had beards. Each man wore a pair of binoculars round his neck on a terribly short strap, and each had a huge bag hanging from his shoulder, containing a telescope for looking at birds too far away for binoculars.

"Much about?" the first one asked Bob.

"Black tern," Bob told them. "Spoonbill."

"Spoonbill!" said the man in a hushed tone. "Wow! That'll be a megatick, that will. I heard there was crane."

"Warden told me they hadn't been seen for more than a week," said Bob. "But never mind – you can see spoonbill from the Tower hide overlooking the Mere. A long way off – but you can see them quite clearly with a telescope."

"Can you see the Trench from there? I'd heard that was the place for curlew sandpiper."

"Not from the Tower. But there's a hide for the Trench just five minutes' walk away."

"Brill!" said the man. "Cheers." He marched off with his followers.

Bob grinned. "Twitchers," he explained to McCann. "The kind of bird-watching fanatic who travels round Britain trying to see new species, and ticking them off their list. They have their own special slang. A tick means the first time they have seen a bird, a megatick means the bird they are seeing for the first time is really special and exciting – like a spoonbill."

"Or a pied kingfisher," offered McCann.

Bob laughed. "That would be a real megatick if you ever saw one of those in Britain. No one ever will, though. Remember how we saw them on the telegraph wires in Sri Lanka?"

As they approached the hut, another man joined them. He looked, from head to toe, the typical twitcher: beard huge, binoculars huger, and on a strap so short you wondered how he got them round his neck. He had an anorak, covered in mud, and wore a woolly hat covered in little badges collected from bird reserves all over the country. An absolutely colossal telescope bag hung from his shoulder.

"Morning mates," he said in a cheerful cockney voice. "Had a good day then, eh? Nice day for it, anyway."

Bob agreed, and told him about black tern and spoonbill. "Saw spoonbill a couple of days ago at Bidsmere," the man offered. "But they'd still be a megatick today." He opened the door to the warden's hut and said: "After you, gents."

The hut was new, and smelt pleasantly of wood. It was decorated with a few bird photographs, typed lists, charts and a large, detailed map of the reserve. "Morning again, warden, me old mate," said the twitcher. "Got a permit from you in the name of Harrison. You got my change yet?"

The warden was a big man dressed in a navy-blue Guernsey, thick corduroy trousers and, naturally, wellingtons. "Uh?" he said. "Oh. I remember. Mr Harrison. You gave me a ten-pound note."

"That's right, me old cock, a tenner it was."

"I've got some change in my jacket – but I left that in my car. Sorry, hang on here, I'll go and fetch it." He turned to McCann and Bob, who were busy studying one of the typed lists. "Enjoy it?"

"Very much," said Bob. "You run the place beautifully."

"It's a miracle we ever got started," said the warden. "All those objections. Trouble isn't over yet in my opinion. And just now, I'm worried sick that some idiot will accidentally start a fire, with the place so dry. Sorry, Mr Harrison, your change. Hang on. Here, have a cigarette." He delved in his pocket and offered cigarettes all round.

"No thanks," said Harrison. "I never touch tobacco."

"Wise man," said the warden, and went out of the hut to fetch the change. Harrison joined Bob and McCann in peering at the lists.

"Did you enjoy the place, then?" asked McCann curiously.

There was something about the way McCann spoke that startled Bob. He had heard his uncle ask innocent questions in that tone of voice before. It generally meant no good to the person he talked to.

But Harrison had noticed nothing. "Great place, yeah, great. Really neat seeing those crane today, big flock of them."

McCann continued, in the same quiet, silky tone: "But you missed spoonbill? You could see them on the far side of the Mere."

"Too far away, had a look through my binoculars but couldn't see them properly. Shame."

"You can't have missed the Tower, though, it's the best spot on the reserve, isn't it Bob?"

"Sure is matey, sure is," said Harrison. "Great view of the Trench, ain't there?"

"Hm," said McCann. "The warden certainly does a fine job in making the reserve attractive to unusual birds."

Harrison grinned: "What's so difficult about that then, eh? Just let the place go wild a bit and they'll flock in. Take my back garden. I'm not much of a gardener, let it go a bit, and what happens? Pair of pied kingfishers come and live there. Come back every summer to nest, they do. I should be a warden myself – not bad, eh?"

"Very impressive," said McCann drily.

The door opened, and the warden came back in. "Here's the man with me nine notes," said Harrison cheerily.

"Frightfully sorry," said the warden, handing the money over. "Here, nine pounds." He rummaged in his pocket and helped himself to a cigarette. "Blast it," he said. "Now I've left my matches in the car."

They all smiled, and Harrison said quickly: "Don't worry mate, I've got a light." He produced a box of matches and lit the warden's cigarette. "Well, cheerio then, mates, I'll be off then. I'm on me bike."

"Mind if I take a look at your telescope before you go?" asked McCann.

Bob looked at his uncle in surprise. But Harrison looked as if he had just been given an electric shock. "Not now," he snapped, and then grinned, with an effort. "Sorry, cock, some other time."

"But I insist," said McCann, and stepped forward to seize the telescope bag.

The result was startling. Harrison leapt back violently and swung the bag with all his force at McCann, who doubled up in pain. "After him Bob," gasped the detective, as Harrison took flight, shoving the startled warden against the wall, flinging the door wide open and sprinting through it.

Bob took off, but bumped into the warden who was staggering forward. He disentangled himself and burst through the door, just in time to see Harrison turn – not towards the car park, but back into the reserve itself.

Bob tore off after him, his binoculars thudding against his chest, as Harrison sprinted down the high narrow pathways lined with tinder-dry grasses. He had such a good start, that for a moment Bob thought he had lost his man, but then he saw a small flock of birds take to the air in alarm – this was no moment to try and identify them – and Bob knew what direction Harrison had taken.

He turned right, and saw Harrison twenty metres ahead, no longer running, but squatting on the ground, the telescope bag before him – and to Bob's utter horror, a box of matches in his hand.

Bob didn't hesitate. He knew Harrison was too far away to stop, and so he plucked his binoculars from round his neck and whirled them round his head two or three times like a cowboy preparing to throw a lasso – and then, with a determined heave, he sent his beautiful and expensive Japanese binoculars flying through the air – straight at Harrison.

Bob had thrown well. The binoculars crashed into Harrison's hand, sending the matches flying the instant before he was about to strike them, and then all at once, Bob was on top of him, pinning him to the ground, the stench of something extremely familiar filling his nostrils.

Petrol.

McCann and the warden appeared at the end of the path: "It's all over," said Bob. "I've got him."

"Well done," said McCann, and he meant it. He helped Bob up, and slapped a pair of handcuffs onto Harrison. "Petrol in a flask in the telescope bag, I suppose?"

"Right," said Bob. The warden looked horror-struck.

"But what?" he gasped. "How?"

McCann explained: "He was going to use the petrol to set fire to the bird reserve. He wanted to destroy it. Why, Harrison?"

Harrison did not look ashamed. He looked furious. "Because this place should be properly developed, not left for the rotten birds. It should have been a power boat centre, and I would have made my fortune selling engines to rich sportsmen. Instead there's nothing here but stupid, horrible birds."

"But why did you go back to the warden? You might have got away with it," Bob asked.

There was a silence. Then Harrison said: "Wanted to get my nine quid back, didn't I?"

"Money's rather been your downfall, hasn't it, Harrison?" said McCann.

There was a very long pause. The warden said: "Thank goodness I'm absent-minded, and forgot his change. But you – you're amazing, Mr McCann! How – how did you know that this man was out to destroy the reserve?"

"Simple," said McCann. "He came to the reserve pretending to be a twitcher – but he didn't get away with it, because he just happened to make six very foolish mistakes."

"That put an end to the phoney twitcher's career, said Bob. "And he's not the first phoney who's had his wings clipped by a bird-watching detective called McCann!"

Did you spot the six mistakes?
Check your answers on page 76.

BIRD PATROL

Thanks to the Blue Peter Bird Patrol we've had a fantastic selection of wild birds feeding in our garden during the winter. Here's how the boys and girls of Bentworth Primary School mounted their campaign.

Last winter, we had to face the fact that over the years we'd been amazingly *unsuccessful* in luring wild birds to the Blue Peter garden! Our nest boxes had never been used, and the only birds we'd spotted were sparrows. Our friend Peter Holden, who runs the RSPB's Young Ornithologists' Club, gave us a few tips.

"The nest box you're using now just isn't working in this sheltered part of your vegetable garden," he said. "I'm afraid that the fact the box is also a bird table is putting the nest builders off. Why not change your tactics – use it just as a bird table and move it to a more open space!" But that

Peter Holden of the Young Ornithologists' Club launched Bird Patrol and helped Sarah, Paul and Shaza position their peanut feeders.

BLUE PETER BIRD PATROL
Stephen Neale
Stephen Neale
Valid until April 1984

BLUE PETER BIRD PATROL
Nada Ramaal
Nada Ramaal
Valid until April 1984

BLUE PETER BIRD PATROL
Paul Plumridge
Paul Plumridge
Valid until April 1984

BLUE PETER BIRD PATROL
Elliott Payne
Elliott Payne
Valid until April 1984

BLUE PETER BIRD PATROL — Tara Burden — Valid until April 1984

BLUE PETER BIRD PATROL — Ali Al Abbassi — Valid until April 1984

Nada, James, Elliott and Courttia helped me fill the hopper with unsalted peanuts, and put kitchen scraps on the table.

wasn't all. "Don't leave anything to chance," Peter advised. "If you have lots of feeding stations in the garden, with lots of different types of food put out regularly, you're bound to attract a variety of birds."

The problem was how on earth could we establish a regular pattern? There's nothing regular about Blue Peter! We're always dashing off to film all over the country, and Peter said the feeding stations had to be stocked up every two or three days without fail. Luckily he came up with the perfect answer.

Schools can join the YOC as well as individuals, and just around the corner from TV Centre, the Bentworth Primary School YOC members agreed to form a Blue Peter Bird Patrol. So far, it's been a tremendous success. From December to the end of March, rain, snow or shine, the Patrol made regular feeding visits and kept our four feeding stations well stocked. Their Blue Peter Log Book makes fascinating reading – not only because it lists the different birds the Patrol spotted, but because of the excellent illustrations – mostly drawn by Ali Al-Abbassi.

Thanks to the Bird Patrol and Peter Holden, we've seen more wild birds in our garden in four months than during the past ten years!

The Bird Patrol kept a record of their sightings in this log book – complete with illustrations!

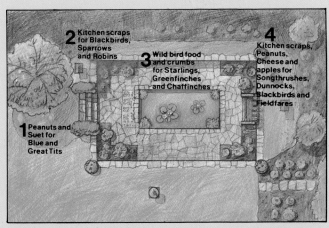

2 Kitchen scraps for Blackbirds, Sparrows and Robins
3 Wild bird food and crumbs for Starlings, Greenfinches and Chaffinches
4 Kitchen scraps, Peanuts, Cheese and apples for Songthrushes, Dunnocks, Blackbirds and Fieldfares
1 Peanuts and Suet for Blue and Great Tits

The four Feeding Stations were masterminded by Peter Holden, and the food put out was designed to appeal to a wide variety of birds.

❋**STOP PRESS** On June 5th we discovered great tits were nesting in this box!

BLUE PETER BIRD PATROL — Courttia Newland — Valid until April 1984

WATCH THE BIRDIE!

Stephen Neale and Courttia Newland of the Bird Patrol lent Eric and me a hand with building the hide. The metal telescopic frame was useful, but you could easily substitute garden canes or dowling.

The cover was canvas with a hole for the camera lens and an entrance flap at the back.

This bluetit and greenfinch were two of Eric's best photos.

One of the world's top bird photographers, Eric Hosking, and his son David, showed us how to set up two interesting experiments. The hide, on the left, and the remote control camera, on the right, » both produced some stunning shots.

Positioning the food in front of David's radio controlled stills camera and the small video camera linked to the monitor in our studio.

A transmitter outside the studio sent a radio pulse to the camera and released the shutter.

We sat in comfort, watching the birds on the monitor and pressing the remote control button when ever we wanted a photo!

A selection of our photos – not bad for armchair photography!

DUNKING DUNCAN

Flying has an odd effect on people. There are some who believe that every flight they make is going to be their last and say goodbye to the world the moment they fasten their seat belts. But the vast majority think that an air crash, like death, is something that happens to other people.

The professional flyers in the Services take the realistic view that they might well be involved in a crash because they are going to be flying in extremely hazardous conditions. This is especially true for helicopter pilots, who are often in dangerous rescue bids over heavy seas. If a helicopter's engines fail over water, the pilot can still put his aircraft down on the surface where it will ride on its floats, giving the crew enough time to escape. But what if the helicopter crashes into the sea out of control and turns over underwater with the pilot stuck in the cabin? To discover the answer to that terrifying question, I went to the Underwater Escape Unit at Portsmouth.

I got kitted out in a dry suit, a life-jacket that didn't work, and a damp, smelly helmet.

It is the most unlikely-looking building which consists of a large tin shed supported on scaffolding 25 metres in the air. I joined a crew from RAF Odiham with several Royal Naval crews who were going through the one-day survival course. We all filed in to the lecture room where Chief Air Crewman Watson, armed with slides of crashed helicopters, took us through the drill.

"When the dunker turns upside down in the tank, this is the view you will have from the cockpit." He smiled, clicked the slide projector, and an indistinguishable mass of dark-blue swirls appeared on the screen. But there were not a lot of laughs from the class, who, apart from me, were all experienced pilots. The "dunker" is a square black box with a simulated cockpit at the front. Huge arms lower the box into a tank of water which slowly revolves until the whole thing is upside down. There were, I was relieved to note, two divers in the water in case anything went wrong with the machinery, or more probably, the nerve of the victim.

"Panic," said Chief Watson, "is your most dangerous enemy."

I could feel the panic beginning already! And it didn't get any better when I realised what I was going to wear for the Test.

"There's your life-jacket," said Petty Officer John Heightley. "Oh good!" I said.

It doesn't work, of course, because you'd never get out of your cockpit wearing an inflated life-jacket.

"And the helmet." He passed me a heavy, damp, smelly bone dome.

I struggled into the cockpit, feeling that I was to swimming what an elephant is to flying.

The seat belt was the final straw. "To release the seat belt – hit the centre clasp and turn clockwise or anticlockwise.

"Orientation point is here," he said, clouting a hand-hold above the door. This, I discovered, was very useful, because when you're upside down in the dark, an orientation hand-hold tells you which way to swim for safety.

"Do *not* release your seat belt until the aircraft has stopped moving." The dunker began to move out to the middle of the tank, with the swimmers hanging on to the side.

I climbed down to the dunker where I was strapped in like a trussed chicken.

I tried to remember how to release my seat belt and which way to swim for the surface as the dunker slowly began to sink beneath the water.

"Standby – Dunking – Now!" The door flew off and the water began to surge into the cockpit. Thankfully, I saw the diver pointing to the hand-hold and grabbed it just in time. The water was now over my thighs and creeping up my body.

"Remember your worst enemy is panic," I thought when the dunker began to turn as the water reached my throat. I took a gulp of air – and I was under. Silence ... The dunker was still turning. My lungs were beginning to burst and my mind started to race ... It must stop now ... Maybe it's gone wrong and isn't going to stop ... If I don't breathe soon, I'll die ... Must get out ... Release the belt ... Out of the harness ... Which way do I go? Am I going the wrong way? Is this the bottom of the tank? AIR!

At last I broke the surface to hear Chief Watson berating me for releasing my seat belt before the aircraft had stopped moving. "In a real crash, if you try to jump out with the helicopter rolling on top of you – you'll never see the surface," he yelled.

The next time it was better. I didn't panic because I knew what was going to happen. I waited until the last second before holding my breath, and let it go very slowly, a bit at a time, until the dunker stopped moving. Then I released the seat belt, rolled over, and struck out for the surface.

They save the worst bit for the end. Up to now we'd been working in the light, but the last dunk was to be in the dark.

A helicopter is just as likely to crash on a moonless night as in broad daylight, so they turned out all the lights and made us drop black visors over our eyes.

"Anybody breaking the surface with his visor up will have it all to do again," warned Chief Watson.

It was really terrifying. I couldn't see a thing, but I could feel the water creeping up my body. I kept my right hand firmly on the orientation hand-hold, took my breath as I felt the water touch my chin and waited for the dunker to stop. Belt off – Go! I felt my bone dome hit the roof of the cockpit. I wasn't out – and I'd let go the orientation hand-hold! Where was I?

At last I was moving – but where to?

"Lights!" I heard Chief Watson call.

Suddenly – with everlasting gratitude – I was back in the world of light, and out of what must be the nearest thing to hell on earth.

I won't say that I actually enjoyed the experience, but I was very glad to have done it.

Chief Watson gave me a certificate when it was all over, and I have stuck it up on my bedroom wall. It is not just that I am proud of the achievement, but it is there to remind me that when things are at their darkest, if I don't panic, it is going to be light again when I reach the surface.

The claxons sounded and the water began to creep slowly up my body. I've never felt more alone in my life.

The water closed over my head. I held my breath and waited for the dunker to stop moving. It seemed an eternity.

I released the seat belt and struck out for the surface. This was the sweetest gulp of air I've ever breathed.

JACK ★ MEETS ★ HIS ★ MATCH

1984 saw the sixth regeneration of Dr Who, as Colin Baker replaced Peter Davison. When the new Doctor visited Blue Peter, he had an amazing effect on Jack. Without so much as a twitch of a whisker, our disappearing cat sat contentedly in the Doctor's arms.

Colin wears a cat brooch on his *Dr Who* coat – he's very fond of all animals – cats in particular, so maybe Jack felt the friendly vibrations.

But perhaps Jack's reaction had something to do with the fact that before our very eyes, he crossed the frontiers of Space and Time when the Doctor magic-ed him in and out of the Tardis!

UPSTAIRS & DOWNSTAIRS

AT
HAM HOUSE

If you visit a stately home, you probably try to imagine what life was like for the rich lords and ladies who lived in the grand rooms, and to guess how many servants were needed to keep them well fed and warm and comfortable.

I was able to see what life was like, upstairs *and* downstairs, in a splendid mansion not ten miles from the Blue Peter studios. It is called Ham House, and three hundred and fifty years ago, William Murray became the owner in a very strange way.

In those days, children who misbehaved or didn't work hard at their lessons were beaten – often quite hard; but it wasn't thought right for royal children to be beaten by

William Murray was given Ham House by King Charles I.

Elizabeth Murray made Ham House a show place.

mere tutors or nurses, so an ordinary child acted as a stand-in. His job was to be beaten when the Royal Prince was in trouble, and he was called a whipping-boy.

The whole system seems dreadfully unfair, but William Murray was whipping-boy for Prince Charles, the son of King James of England and Scotland. Fortunately, Prince Charles was usually good, so William didn't have too bad a time, and the boys were friends. When Charles grew up, he became King Charles I, and rewarded his

whipping-boy by making him an Earl, with enough money to buy Ham House. And because he had no son, King Charles arranged that his daughter succeed to the title, and to Ham House.

Her name was Elizabeth, and she was very striking to look at, with marvellous red hair. Unfortunately, red hair was very unfashionable, and was even considered ugly, so her portraits all make her hair look fairer and less red than it really was.

Elizabeth Murray loved Ham House, and determined to make it

one of the greatest houses in England. For her second husband, she married the Duke of Lauderdale, who was enormously rich, and was ready to spend a fortune making Ham House a show place.

Together they designed and planned and furnished lavish, rich rooms, and beautiful gardens stretching down to the River Thames. The kitchens had to be perfect, too. Under Ham House lay not only a kitchen, but two larders, a scullery, a dairy, a bakehouse, a still house for making preserves, four cellars for beer and wine, a Servants' Hall and a laundry! Years later, long after the last of the family had died, the house was thrown open to the public, and thousands of people visited the beautiful state rooms, but the kitchens were sadly neglected.

That was until 1984. Now they are completely restored so that you can see what life was like downstairs as well as upstairs, when the red-haired Duchess of Lauderdale reigned at Ham House. Caroline Davidson, an expert in the history of cooking, told me of her detective work to find old kitchen equipment, like a spit jack for roasting meat, and how she'd shown modern craftsmen how to make things that had vanished for ever – like three-hundred year old brooms and an egg-whisk made from twigs.

Caroline had even reproduced – in plaster and plastic – the kind of food that would have been found in the kitchen all those years ago – delicacies like a fish pie holding a whole salmon caught in the Thames that morning, and a bride pie, with six different fillings, one of them a live snake – a seventeenth century practical joke!

Caroline Davidson, an expert on the history of cooking, who supervised the restoration of the kitchens.

The kitchen is so realistic, it looks as if the servants have only just left. If you shut your eyes, it's easy to imagine what life must have been like for the kitchen maids, with the housekeeper and cook shouting their orders.

"Janet, hurry up, girl – Bring those cabbages! – Where's the flour? – Stir that broth! – Get on with washing the dishes! – Sweep that floor!"

The next time I use my electric mixer and shove the dirty pots in the dishwasher – I'll spare a thought for the kitchen maids at Ham House, beating their eggs with a handful of twigs, and slaving over the huge stone sinks!

P.S. After my visit to Ham House had been shown on *Blue Peter*, we had a letter from Mrs Lily Johnson who had actually been a kitchen-maid at Ham House 49 years ago! She said:

Dear Janet,
I watched the 'Blue Peter' programme with great interest today. When you pretended to be a 17th century kitchen-maid! I really was at Ham House in 1935-ish. Truth is stranger than fiction. Probably the last kitchen-maid there and I didn't consider I have used the mortar & pestle exhibited. The hours were long but stuff were a happy work hard because we unit. Each had our own work I scrubbed the long table, floors and woodwork daily, as well as preparing vegetables, skinning rabbits, hares & plucking pheasants, grouse and woodcock in season. I used with other servants to swim in the Thames when off duty. As my pay was only £30 a year & all found as the term was. (Payable three monthly) We mainly had to find our own entertainment i.e. walking, reading etc money scarce. I still swim every week at sixty-four & it certainly didn't do me any harm (the long hours) more interesting Wishing you lots of future.
Sincerely
(Mrs) L. M. Johnson.

17th Century kitchen maids had a hard life!

"EXCELLENT SMALL CAKES"

Here's your chance to try out a genuine 17th-century recipe – a top favourite from the Ham House kitchen. In 1669, the cook made enough to feed a small army, so Caroline Davidson scaled the ingredients down for a 20th-century family!

Ingredients for 27 cakes

8 oz (225 g) plain flour
2 oz (50 g) white sugar
2 oz (50 g) soft brown sugar
8 oz (225 g) currants (soaked in water for 1½ hrs then patted dry with kitchen roll)
4 oz (125 g) unsalted butter
1 egg yolk (size 3)
1 tablespoon single cream (or top of the milk)
1 tablespoon sherry
(or 1 tablespoon water and a few drops of vanilla essence)
½ teaspoon grated nutmeg
Icing sugar for dusting

Method

1 Sieve the flour into a bowl and rub in butter with fingertips until the mixture is like breadcrumbs – a good tip is to cut the butter into small pieces first.

2 Add the sugar, nutmeg and currants (you can use sultanas or small raisins, too).

3 Put the egg yolk, single cream (or top of the milk), sherry (or water and vanilla essence) into a small bowl and mix well.

4 Work liquid into main mixture until it forms a thick paste – this takes time!

5 Put paste on floured board and knead until smooth. Roll out to ½ cm thick and cut out cakes using a glass or cup with a 7 cm diameter rim.

6 Place on a baking sheet, prick each cake well with a fork to roughen up the surfaces and bake in the centre of the oven, Gas Mark 4, 180°C/350°F, for 20–25 minutes until pale, golden brown.

7 Whilst still hot, dust with icing sugar and remove cakes with a fish slice onto a wire rack to cool.

WONDER DOG JUDY

The story of the First Lady of the Gun Boats – Judy, RN – the only dog who was an official Prisoner of War, and who won the Animals' VC.

1 Nearly fifty years ago, in 1936, a female pointer puppy was born in Shanghai. Her Chinese kennel maid called her Shu-di, which means peaceful, so her English owners called her Judy – but Judy was to lead anything but a peaceful life.

2 When she grew up Judy was bought by the officers and men of *HMS Gnat,* a tiny gunboat patrolling the troubled waters of the Yangtze River. Soon she made friends with all the ship's company.

3 Once she crawled through the guard rails and fell into the fast-running river. The Captain called "Man Overboard!" A boat was lowered, and Judy was dragged back to safety – this was the first of her narrow escapes. Two years later Judy left China.

4 Britain and Japan were at war. Judy and her friends were ordered to sail to Singapore, and Judy became the ship's plane spotter and early-warning system. She would look up in the sky and bark whenever she heard Japanese bombers approaching.

5 When they reached Singapore, they found the city smouldering from air attacks and women and children fleeing from the advancing Japanese troops.

6 Soon Judy's ship was crowded with refugees hoping to escape. The children were frightened and miserable, and Judy tried hard to cheer them up.

7 When the bombers attacked the refugee ships, the survivors struggled for the shore – but Judy was nowhere to be seen.

8 Later, when a volunteer swam back to the wreck in search of food and bedding, he heard a strange whining – and there was Judy, trapped by the wreckage, but unhurt. "I've found Judy!" he yelled to the survivors ashore.

9 A party set out to cross the island of Sumatra to try and reach the port of Padang ahead of the Japanese. They had to force their way through hot and humid jungle filled with mosquitoes and snakes. For five weeks Judy walked with them. She was the Chief Guard and Water Finder of the expedition.

10 But it was no use – the Japanese had captured Padang. Now they were all prisoners of war and were put into prison camps. The Japanese guards despised men who were taken prisoner; they treated them with great cruelty and gave them very little food.

11 It was here Judy met the man who was to be her master for the rest of her life. His name was Frank Williams, and he had been in the RAF before he had been taken prisoner. He gave Judy part of his precious ration of rancid boiled rice, and she would go ratting and bring him her catch. The prisoners were so desperate they were glad to eat rats.

12 Judy was able to get out of the camp, and one day she had a litter of puppies. Frank gave one to the Camp Commander as a present for his girl-friend, and in return, he made Judy an official prisoner of war.

13 So Judy became the only dog ever to be listed as an official Prisoner of War. She was entitled to a handful of rice a day and the men managed to make her a collar and disc with a scrap of tin and old rope.

14 But when the prisoners were ordered to be shipped from Padang they were told to leave Judy behind, so Frank trained her to lie still for hours in an old sack so that he could smuggle her on board.

15 The derelict old prison ship was torpedoed. 500 of the 700 prisoners were killed – the rest struggled in the dangerous, shark-ridden water.

16 Frank saw Judy helping a man to reach a floating piece of wood he could cling on to. Then she deliberately went back to help someone else. Judy saved the lives of four men on that dreadful day.

17 Then the worst thing of all happened. The men were sent *back* to Sumatra to build a railway through the jungle. They were used as slave labour, cutting trees, clearing sites, and dragging heavy rails and sleepers. They were kept on starvation rations, working ten and twelve hours a day. Dreadful illness ravaged them, but there were no drugs or medical supplies.

18 Soon the men were like skeletons, half their normal weight, and Judy was scrawny, emaciated, and covered with sores. But as long as Frank staggered on, she kept beside him. One of the prisoners wrote a verse about her:

"They would stagger to their work place
Though they really ought to die,
And would mutter in their beards
'If that bitch can, so can I'!"

19 The prisoners lost all count of time, but one day no Japanese guards appeared. A handful of men entered the camp – they came from the British Parachute Regiment. The war was over – Japan had surrendered. At last the prisoners of war were free.

20 Soon they were back in Singapore, ready to board a troopship to take them home! A large notice said: "No dogs or pets of any kind to be taken aboard". "You're not a dog," Frank said to Judy. "You're a Prisoner of War. Come along!" So they went aboard and Judy was given permission to land in England.

21 Now she found she was a famous heroine. She was awarded the Dickin Medal, which is given to brave animals, and is sometimes called the Animals' VC. Her citation read: "For magnificent courage and endurance in Japanese Prison Camps, thus helping to maintain morale among her fellow prisoners, and for saving many lives by her intelligence and watchfulness.

FOUR-IN-HAND

The cones formed a gap only 30 cm wider than the carriage.

There are few sights more splendid, stately or peaceful than a carriage-and-four trotting down a country lane. It wasn't until I saw the Duke of Edinburgh on Grandstand turning a carriage over in the middle of a river that I realised that the sport of carriage driving was not quite so sedate as I had imagined.

To find out more about it, Goldie and I set off for Windsor to meet Peter Munt who is the Number 2 Whip in the world.

Peter, middle-aged, wearing a long-sleeved jersey, a tie and a brown trilby hat, with a Jack Russell at his heels, doesn't look any more of a tearaway than the Duke of Edinburgh. He speaks with a soft, Buckinghamshire burr and moves like a countryman – as Biddy Baxter says I do – deliberately, but not in a hurry. Goldie and Buster, the Jack Russell, leapt up on the back of the carriage, and Peter slid into the driver's seat with me by his side. Peter told me he was taught to drive by his father when he was 8 years old, so there was no doubting that I was in experienced hands and it is in the hands that the skill of carriage driving lies. Peter handed me the reins.

"Now you've got to feel that carriage behind you – and when the horses aren't going right, you correct them – inch by inch. Let's see how you get on through the cones."

"How do you stop them if they head for the lake?" I asked.

"There's a brake beneath your foot – but you concentrate on turning them."

"Walk on!" I said and immediately, Boujeon and Callan began to move. I discovered the delicacy that was needed to control them. The slightest touch sent them to the left or right, and I felt the carriage swing behind me.

"Gently now – don't let them rush you! Feel them round – bring them back a little bit. That's right – talk to them, Simon."

The horses respond to the voice as much as the rein, and like humans, they need a lot of encouragement.

The cones form a gap 30 centimetres wider than the carriage – and with tight 90° turns, you need every scrap of concentration to get through.

On the first round I had something else that's necessary for all sportsmen – luck! Peter couldn't believe that I'd actually gone clear, with not a single cone nudged.

"You've got me a bit worried, so we'd better go again," he said with a wry smile.

My confidence was high this time, but the skill seemed to have gone with my luck. I concentrated just as much, and began to get the feel of the horses, but I demolished every cone on the circuit.

"What went wrong?" I asked.

Peter smiled encouragingly. "It was very nice, Simon – but you didn't quite judge it, did you?"

So far we had only driven two-in-hand, and along reasonably respectable tracks, but when we returned to the stables, Sarah Felgate, Peter's chief groom, was waiting for us with two more magnificent greys who were going to make up our four.

Goldie and Buster kept their balanc the back as I daringly put on a spurt – and demolished a c

My teachers – Peter Munt and his chief groom, Sarah Felgate.

Driving four-in-hand requires even more skill – there's an awful lot of horse between you and the leaders!

Apart from the complications of controlling four spirited horses, I was now occupying much more space on the road.

Whilst I helped Sarah with the harnessing, Peter explained the difference between the carriage I had been driving and the cross-country carriage.

"It's short and narrow, and it's made of iron. If the horses can get through, then so can the carriage. And if you do hit something, it's so solid you'll bounce off it."

I climbed up beside Peter and took hold of the reins. There seemed an awful lot of horse between me and the leaders.

"Take all four reins in your left hand, and then you pick whichever rein you want with your right, depending on which way you want to turn."

It felt very different from driving with a pair. Apart from the complications of controlling four spirited horses, I was now occupying much more space on the road.

We paused before turning into country, so that I could get into the back with Sarah, whilst Peter picked up the reins.

"You hold on to this bar at all times – and try not to get your fingers trapped," Sarah told me.

"What happens if we fall out?" I asked.

"We don't. We're not allowed to fall out," she said.

Sarah was a pretty girl with longish hair, and wearing a man's cap which added a dash of style.

We trotted over a field towards a dense-looking copse, which I thought we were going to skirt round,

but with a slight touch on the leading rein, we plunged through the bracken and scythed in and out of gaps between trees, which I would never have risked in a Land-Rover.

"Get over to the right," called Peter, and Sarah and I hung over the edge like ocean-going yacht racers.

"Now left – come on Boujeon – move boy!"

We suddenly graunched to a stop before a very narrow gap between two towering trees which Boujeon didn't fancy at all. Quick as a flash, Sarah was off the back and shoving Boujeon's huge flank through the gap. Then we were off again, with Sarah bounding back on to the carriage as we flashed through the trees and down towards the river at breakneck speed.

There was not the slightest hesitation from the horses, who leapt into the torrent, up to their hocks in swirling water, the carriage making great bow waves as we roared through the river and charged up the bank on the other side.

Peter let me have the reins again as we cantered along the home stretch, looking as we did at the beginning, like a stately picture on a Christmas card. When I contemplated my bruises in the bath that night, I decided that carriage driving was perhaps not quite the right sport for those who enjoy a nice, quiet ride through the countryside!

GIANT RED DRAGON

Question:
What do monster-sized foam rubber sausages, giant mushrooms and bouncing buns have in common?

Answer:
They were all ideas for our competition to design a garden for Liverpool's International Garden Festival.

Three months after Theo's plan for a dragon won our competition, he was shaking hands with the Queen at the Opening of the International Garden Festival!

Everything about the Festival is colossal! The site covers a massive 125 acres. Two and a half years ago it was an enormous rubbish dump and a million and a quarter tons of rubble had to be cleared, before even a blade of grass could be planted. And last January when Goldie and I travelled to Merseyside to see the plot of land reserved for Blue Peter, I must admit, my heart sank! How on earth could a boring, flat triangle of mud possibly be transformed into anything attractive?

Blue Peter viewers came up with 19,940 ideas! We never dreamed we'd receive such imaginative and well-thought out suggestions. A baked bean stepping stone path was the main feature of a Sausage & Mash Garden; another idea was for huge computer games. There was a plan for a garden based on the games compendium that we'd just shown on the programme, and a magnificent water-dome, as high as a 3-storey house, scored high marks from the judges for inventiveness.

In the end, though, 14-year old Theo Gayer Anderson's Giant Red Dragon was such a brilliant idea, we were unanimous in making it Overall Top Winner.

But how do you set about building a dragon 20 metres long with a massive 40 metre mouth? Theo and I soon discovered when we visited the site – and were set to work! A dragon-shaped mound of earth was covered with netting. The whole thing was spread with concrete and painted in the vivid colours shown in Theo's plan. The head, with its fearsome, gnashing teeth, was specially moulded in a factory.

On May 2nd, Theo, Goldie and I waited anxiously by our garden entrance for some Very Important Visitors. Her Majesty the Queen, accompanied by the Duke of Edinburgh, was opening the Festival and much to our delight, she had agreed to look at our Dragon on her whistle-stop Festival tour. Hours earlier, while we were taking shots of the garden on video to show on Blue Peter the next day, sniffer dogs inspected every corner of the 125-acre site. Goldie was keenly interested in the business-like looking labrador who sniffed us out! Most of the casual-looking passers-by turned out to be security guards, and the

The dragon builders! A mound of earth had to be spread with netting before it was covered in concrete and painted. Rodney Beaumont, the Festival's Design Co-ordinator, masterminded the plan.

helicopter buzzing overhead was a police spotter plane!

Then the chuff-chuff-chuff of the model steam railway drew closer – there was a hiss of steam as it stopped, followed by a deafening clicking as hundreds of press photographers snapped away. The Royal party walked towards us, and I hoped I wouldn't be tongue-tied.

"This is Theodore Gayer Anderson . . ." I heard the Chairman of Merseyside Development Corporation introduce us – ". . . and Simon Groom of the Blue Peter programme . . ." And there I was, shaking hands with the Queen! She seemed very intrigued by our Dragon. "The idea is you walk along his back and slide out of his mouth," explained Theo. "Just the sort of thing Prince William would like," said the Queen. And with a

smile, she was off to the Beatles Maze and the Yellow Submarine.

"Gosh, I was nervous!" said Theo. "Yes, so was I," I replied. But someone wasn't. The next day, a large photo was printed in *The Times* newspaper. It showed me pointing out our dragon to The Queen – and Goldie was busy, too! She was taking an inquisitive sniff at the Royal bouquet!

ORIGAMI

I'll never forget the day Mr Yoshizawa came to the Blue Peter studio. He's Japan's leading Origami master – one of the world's top experts in the art of paper folding, and with a few deft strokes of his fingers, our studio was transformed into a miniature zoo!

With help from pretty Fumi Champman, who acted as our interpreter, I discovered Akira Yoshizawa had been transforming paper into models for over sixty years.

When he was four years old, he was given a small paper boat. His big brother and sister broke it, so he tried to make a new one, and ever since then he's never stopped folding paper.

You really wouldn't think it was possible to produce complicated shapes like gorillas, camels, kangaroos, pandas, dragonflies and beetles from single sheets of

Mr Yoshizawa, from Tokyo, has made thousands of origami models without a single cut or tear – the art lies in the folding!

paper – without a single cut or tear. But we had the proof before our very eyes. You name it – Mr Yoshizawa could make it!

I noticed he lifted his paper in the air when he made his models, and Mr Yoshizawa told me that's the ideal way to fold paper, because you can feel *both* sides with your fingers.

And to prove that you don't cut the paper to make Origami figures, Mr Yoshizawa used real bank-notes for some of his models. They included an elephant made out of a one-thousand-yen note (worth about £2) and he was clever enough to be able to use the different colours of the bank-notes to make the patterns on his models.

It really was magic – a squirrel appeared on a bed of beech leaves, and a swan with three cygnets surrounded by water lilies. His dogs were so good you could even recognise the different breeds – there was a setter, an Airedale, an Alsatian and a husky.

Goldie was an excellent model, but one animal defeated him. You've guessed it – Mr Yoshizawa never got the chance to have a go at a Silver tabby – Jack did his famous disappearing act!

Mr Yoshizawa uses real banknotes for some of his models.

Janet's Jump

It's odd what nerves will make you do. I can remember going to my first interview for Blue Peter and Biddy Baxter saying to me: "If you got this job, what would you like most to do on the programme?" And I suddenly heard myself saying: "I'd love to do a free fall parachute jump."

It had never crossed my mind before, but as I said it, I knew that that was what I wanted to do more than anything else. So – six months later, I found myself at the RAF No. 1 Parachute Training School, suspended from the roof in a parachute harness like a puppet on a string with Sergeant Nigel Rogoff shouting:

"Let's hear it Janet. A thousand and one – a thousand and two – a thousand and check! And you should see your canopy open. If you don't, what do you do?"

"I pull my reserve."

"Good girl!"

Nigel was a member of the RAF Falcons – the best Free Fall display team in the world – so I was in good hands. The Falcons trained John Noakes who created a Blue Peter record by becoming the first civilian to make a 25,000 feet free fall descent in 1973. That record was broken in 1980, and I intend to get it back for Blue Peter.

But there's a lot to learn before you get anywhere near an aeroplane, beginning with how to fall when you hit the ground at 20 mph.

Training began with me suspended from the roof in a parachute harness like a puppet on a string.

My instructor, Sergeant Nigel Rogoff, is a member of the world's best Free Fall team – the RAF Falcons.

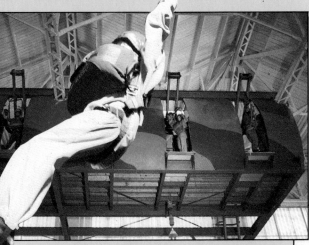

The fan trainer – high in the roof – was my first actual jump.

"Legs together – elbows in – look straight ahead."

This time I was swinging like a pendulum holding on to a ring suspended from the roof.

"Go!"

I let go on the apex of the swing – and hit the mat on the floor of the hanger.

"Keep those elbows in or you'll break your arms, Janet."

"Right – up to the fan trainer."

The fan trainer is the first actual jump. The parachute harness is attached to ropes running through pulleys that slow down your fall just enough to simulate the real thing. Nigel was by my side.

"Right Janet – remember all you've been told,

and that our motto is 'knowledge dispels fear'." His intense blue eyes twinkled. "This is the first time you've got to show a bit of bottle. Take your time. You'll be alright."

He seemed to know instinctively when I needed a gentle word of encouragement or an imperative word of command.

"Go!" The rope whizzed through the pulleys and in three seconds I hit the ground with my legs together – elbows in – and rolling over in the correct position.

The outdoor exit trainer was something else.

Seventy feet from the ground this time – just high enough to give you the real colly-wobbles; it whirls you downwards at a steep angle in jerks and bursts which simulates the slipstream of an aircraft travelling at 160 mph.

Nigel slid back the safety bar and I was poised on the threshold of 70 feet of nothing.

"Action stations position for a starboard exit!" he commanded, and then in a softer voice – with a smile – "and a good drive out, Janet. OK?"

"Red on! Go!"

How could I disobey?

"1001, 1002, 1003, a thousand and check!" I yelled as I was flung through the air like a stunter kite on a windy day.

The first real parachute descent was to be made from a balloon 800 feet from the ground.

Nigel built up my confidence by showing me all the care that was taken in packing my parachute and demonstrating the secure beauty of the canopy when it is open and filled with wind. Finally he showed me exactly what would happen if things went wrong. Every parachutist carries a "reserve" strapped to his chest. On top is a large red handle – to be pulled if your main parachute fails to open.

Nigel made me stand in a mock-up of the balloon cabin with a 2-foot step to the ground.

"Go!" he called.

"1001, 1002, 1003," I shouted.

The outdoor exit trainer was far worse! Standing 70 feet from the ground gave me colly-wobbles!

"You have a malfunction!" Nigel's voice echoed through the hanger. I grabbed the red handle and pulled – and my reserve parachute shot out in an instant. It was kind of reassuring in its terrifying way.

It was cold, and there was a thin drizzle in the air as we walked across to the big, silver balloon. I strapped on my parachute, now with accustomed ease, and stepped into the cabin.

"Can they bring the balloon down again quite quickly?" I asked. Nigel's blue eyes looked straight at me. "It's of no interest to you – because there's only one way you're coming down."

800 feet is unreal enough to take away that awful sickening feeling in the groin and replace it with a numb sense of unreality. The thought that in a few minutes I was going to leap out onto what looked like a map of the area seemed totally ridiculous. Nigel hooked the static line which was going to open my parachute into its bolt.

"You've nothing to worry about. Remember all your drill and enjoy yourself. Step forward – both hands across your reserve. Look up – and good drive out. Go!"

"1001, 1002, 1003 and thousand and check!" – and there, just as Nigel promised, was my beautiful green canopy billowing above my head. I felt that sudden, lovely jerk as my fall was arrested and I began the beautiful drift down to earth. The fear had all gone, and for the first time I was really enjoying myself – the wind on my face, the magnificent panoramic view of the countryside as the little dots began to take shape becoming cars speeding along the road, or cows grazing in a field – and the magnificent silence of it all.

"Janet keep your knees together – you have 10 seconds before landing. Assess your drift."

The peace was broken by Flight Lieutenant Dave Griffiths talking me down through a loud hailer.

"That's a good position now, Janet."

The ground was really hurtling towards me – and the impact, when it came, was much harder than anything I had experienced in training, but I remembered everything Nigel had told me, and apart from a grass burn, I was all in one piece. The feeling of exhilaration was indescribable. It was my very best thing since I joined Blue Peter.

But the Free Fall was still to come.

I'd made it! My parachute, so carefully packed by Senior Aircraft Woman Teresa Young, had stood me in good stead. And thanks to Nigel's training, I hit the dropping zone.

"Semi Frog Position" – those words will be with me to my dying day! But learning how to control your body is absolutely vital for a safe free fall.

Two months later I was back in the training wing and dangling from the roof again, but this time I was in line with the ground learning how to control my body whilst hurtling through space.

"Semi Frog Position," Nigel called up to me, "legs tucked up behind your backside – arms forward and curved round – palms facing the ground."

I could see the ground 6 feet below me – what, I wondered, would it look like 12,000 feet away with nothing to suspend me from the sky!

"Quick glance at your altimeter –

"It is reading 3,000 feet.

"Hand on your main handle . . . Operate your mains!"

I pulled the handle which would have opened my parachute and the simulator jerked me into the vertical position.

"Look up and check your canopy."

I woke up the next day as soon as it was light. I

opened the curtains and peered out. The sun was shining and there wasn't a cloud in the bright, blue sky. 'Gin clear' – as the Falcons would say. I looked at the tree in my garden – only the faintest rustle in the top leaves. It was perfect jumping weather. My first reaction was – "Good we can do it" – but as I drove down the now familiar lane to the training centre, and the great hangers of Abingdon hoved into sight – I thought, what would I give for a leaden sky and force 10 gale – and "Sorry jumping's off for today, Janet!"

But the sun was shining on Nigel's smiling face – and his first words were: "A great day for free falling Janet."

We were going to jump from a Hercules – a huge troop-carrying aircraft with massive rear exit doors.

I began to get into the gear, the straps and buckles now as familiar to my hands as the buttons of my favourite dress.

Parachute on, reserve across my chest, red helmet in my hand, I joined Nigel and the rest of the Falcons to walk across the tarmac towards the waiting aircraft. We trooped on board and sat in a row along the stark metal fusilage. This was no luxury airliner. The boys were chatting about everyday things, which shocked me at first – like gossiping in church – until I realised that free-falling was an everyday thing for them. Only Nigel was silent – he was living through the numb terror he knew was beginning to close in on me. I was his responsibility – his protegé – the first girl to jump with the Falcons. I mustn't let him down.

The Hercules sprang into life and began to vibrate as the engines ran up to speed. "I hate flying," said one of the team as we began to climb. "I never really

The point of no return! Seconds later I was hurtling through space and falling 8,000 feet before my 'chute opened!

next second I was vertical again, feet towards the ground just like the simulator. But this time it was real and there was the sun shining through my lovely green canopy as I began to drift gently towards the ground.

I had fallen free. We hit the dropping zone within seconds of each other and soon Nigel and the boys were all around me. They all asked the same thing. Did you enjoy it?.

"It's really great, isn't it?". I realised that I was being welcomed into a very exclusive club.

You see – for us free fallers – there is nothing quite like it in the world.

"The next one is the big one," said Nigel. "And that really will be something!"

feel safe in an aeroplane." Nigel smiled and turned towards me.

"Now you've got nothing to worry about. You've had the finest training in the world. Just go out there and enjoy yourself. Everybody's rooting for you."

At 12,000 feet the aircraft levelled off – and with a roar that stopped all conversation, the great rear doors gaped open. I have never felt more exposed in my life – it was like standing on the threshold of eternity.

I put my helmet on and walked towards the great white hole. Nigel adjusted my goggles – and then to my surprise, gave me a socking great kiss.

"I'll bet he doesn't do that to every parachutist, I thought – and leapt into space.

My breath was snatched away and I was tumbling head over heels through the sky. "Semi Frog Position – I kept saying to myself. Nigel's words kept coming back – "legs tucked behind your backside – arms curved – palms down facing ground."

And suddenly there was Nigel in the semi frog position, alongside me at 10,000 feet, and smiling as if he was in the hanger at Abingdon! He mouthed something at me, and then he was gone, and I began to spin like a top. I could see the dropping zone flare whirling round beneath as I tried to correct the spin.

Then Nigel appeared again – from out of nowhere. We had planned that he would operate my mains if the automatic opening device should fail.

Were we in an emergency condition? I wondered. But there was a sweet, reassuring jerk as the automatic system released my parachute, and the

How Stupid Can You Get?

It was a shattering sight to see our beautiful Italian Sunken Garden wrecked by vandals – but Blue Peter viewers came to our rescue in the most amazing ways!

It was like someone hitting you in the stomach – hard. The first we heard about it was from the lady at the till in the Television Centre canteen. "Your garden's a dreadful mess," she said. "I looked out of the window and I couldn't believe my eyes."

Members of 33 Squadron from RAF Odiham came to our rescue!

Poisoning our fish with oil was the worst blow, but Brian Banks helped us revive them – miraculously, many survived.

While Simon, Peter and Brian helped the RAF apply the special detergent spray to clear the oil, I gave Percy a hand replanting the small urns with polyanthus and tulips.

We never believed our beautiful antique urn could be restored, but David Salmon achieved the impossible – you can't see a single join!

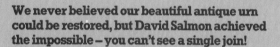

Neither could we. The canteen overlooks the garden – or rather canteens. There are three of them, and it must have been at night when the vandals struck, because during the day they're full of hungry customers. And it must have been at the weekend, too, because this was on Monday and we were busy doing Blue Peter. We'd been out in the garden the previous Thursday, and we'd fed the fish on Friday, so the damage had obviously been done on Saturday or Sunday.

When we dashed outside, a horrible sight met our eyes. The garden looked like a battlefield. The lovely antique garden urn, given to us by Mr Taylor, of Barnet, had been smashed to pieces. It had been in his family for years, and Mr Taylor had very kindly donated it to Blue Peter for safe keeping because he was getting on and was frightened *his* garden might be vandalised!

All our smaller urns at the corners of the garden wall, carefully planted with bulbs and polyanthus by us and Percy, had been up-turned, the contents scattered, and the urns themselves thrown down to the beds below. Our wooden seat was in the pond, and most of the bedding plants had been trampled or uprooted. Our sundial, another present from a viewer, Miss May Butt, of Chingford, had been hauled off its concrete base in the lawn, smashed in half and thrown down to the paving. The gnomon, the metal pointer from the centre of the dial that tells the time of day, was completely missing.

But by far the worst of all was the black, stinking, gooey sludge that covered the paving and the grass and lay like a thick blanket over the pond. The vandals had drenched the garden in *fuel oil* and had even left a half-empty can behind.

We alerted the people in the Blue Peter office, telephoned Percy Thrower and our fish expert, Brian

Banks, and with heavy hearts we set about the rescue operations. We drained the pond, pulling the bodies of the goldfish out. Poisoning the fish, who hadn't done anyone any harm, was the cruelest blow of all.

But to our amazement, one or two of the black blobs began to move when we put them in tanks of clean water. Miraculously, not all the fish were dead.

That afternoon we broke the news to viewers, and showed photos of the dreadful damage. After that, the phones never stopped ringing! We must have had hundreds of calls from people wanting to help. And letters, too, full of kind messages from children and adults who'd had gardens vandalised themselves, and knew just how we felt. We had offers of plants and fish, and even pocket money to help us restock. It was fantastic! "You certainly know who your friends are when you're in trouble," said Simon, and he was absolutely right.

One of the phone calls came from Corporal Taff Lewis, of RAF Odiham, who said that he and six of his mates from 33 Squadron wanted to spend their day off clearing up the mess. So on November 24th, Operation Clean Up began. What with the RAF and Percy and Brian, we had a terrific team, and we started off with Taff and the boys forming a bucket chain to get rid of the revolting, oily slime that was left in the bottom of the pond after it was drained.

Stage two was applying a special detergent spray (selected by Brian as safe for the fish). It had to be squirted on, then thoroughly brushed in, and left for a while before it was hosed off.

Brian said it was vital not just to remove all the slurry from the pond, but to clean the edges, too. "Otherwise,

BBC Commissionaires keep a 24-hour watch on the video that now scans the garden. Powerful floodlights are switched on at night.

when it rains, the water will seep through the paving, taking the oil with it, and pollute the pond all over again," he explained.

Percy and Janet had their work cut out replanting the small urns and cleaning the pond plants. But bit by bit, the transformation took place, and three back-breaking hours later, it was complete. The finished result was magnificent! We couldn't have been more pleased. We'd saved a great many of the fish, and during the pond cleaning, Pete had spotted the gnomon from the sundial, so we knew we'd be able to have that restored, too.

The antique urn was more of a problem – quite honestly, it only looked fit for the dustbin. But Simon had a flash of inspiration – "What about David Salmon?"

"David *who*?" we asked.

"He's one of Britain's top ceramic restorers," he explained. "Five years ago, he mended a plate for us, and you couldn't tell it had ever been broken."

Once again, we were in luck. David agreed to have a go, and now our urn's as good as new. An electronic alarm system has been installed, and our garden's floodlit at night. A 24-hour video camera scans the whole area, too.

And thanks to Percy and Brian, Taff and his mates, Warrant Officer Class II Len Morris REME who mended our sundial, David Salmon – and not forgetting Blue Peter viewers all over Britain, Operation Clean Up was one hundred percent successful!

Thanks to Blue Peter viewers and friends, our garden – complete with Petra's statue and our Tree for the Year 2000 – looks better than ever!

Games Compendium

I like board games. They're good fun if you're at a loose end, and my favourite for a rainy day is roulette. But my eyes popped out on stalks when I saw the roulette wheel in the beautiful "Games Compendium" that came to the studio before it was auctioned at Phillips earlier this year.

Roulette was just one of the sixteen games that all fitted into a polished wooden box made of a rare wood called coromandel. When you opened the lid, two side wings spread out to reveal a mass of small compartments and hidden drawers that were all crammed with games. There were over 380 counters, dice and ivory chess men. There were miniature playing cards and whist markers with carved ivory hands that turned round to keep the score, and carved ivory sticks for the favourite Victorian game of spillikins. A leather chess board folded up and fitted into the lid of the box, and another board, made of coromandel and inlaid with ivory, was for a steeplechase game with a difference – all the horses and the jumps were made from solid silver, decorated with real gold!

The silver monogram on the lid of the box was the initials of the lucky man who owned it. He was Sir Ernest Cassell, the Victorian millionaire, who raced and bred his own horses, so the Steeplechase game was probably his favourite. Phillips thought the Games Compendium, that was made in 1882, might fetch £5000 – it went for more than double! I only hope the new owner enjoys playing with it as much as I did!

Cards

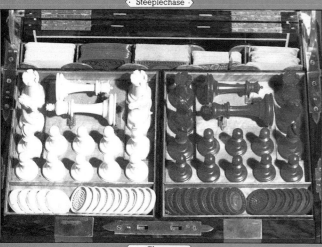

Steeplechase

Chess

Dice & Spinners

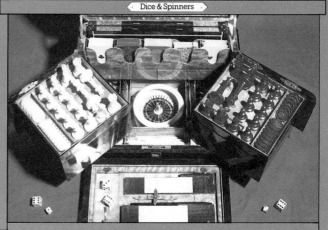

SOLUTIONS

Now find a mirror.

SOLUTIONS

Now find a mirror.

Puzzle Pictures

1 Trying out a **Ball Bath** – a seething mass of 56,000 plastic balls.

2 **The Ebonettes**, New York's top league **Double Dutch** team.

3 Another bathing sensation – air pumped through hundreds of tiny holes produces millions of bubbles to tone up your muscles.

4 **Colin Chinnery** from Edinburgh, the only boy in Britain learning the ancient art of **Shaolin** in China.

5 The greatest footballer of all time – Edson Arantes de Nascimento **Pelé**.

6 **Felix the Cat** – the famous cartoon character of the 1920s.

7 **Bryn Owen's Super Scooter** customised with 87 lamps and 36 rear view mirrors.

8 Captured by a **Cyberman** during our **Dr Who 20th Anniversary** celebrations.

9 Centurion Simonius Groomus with some of the 10,000 Roman soldiers – part of the celebrations for **Lincoln's 2,100th birthday.**

10 Olympic medalist **Neil Adams** warmed us up with his training routine.

11 The world's first **large-scale sponsored Dog Sit!**

12 **The Goodies** provide all the voices for the **Bananaman** cartoons.

The case of the Twitcher's Telescope

1 Harrison was pretending to be a "twitcher," or bird-watching fanatic – but he got his twitcher's slang wrong. McCann first became suspicious when Harrison said that spoonbill would be a megatick when he saw them for the second time. As Bob had explained to McCann, a bird is only a megatick when seen for the first time.

2 Harrison said he had seen crane – but McCann already knew from the warden that the crane had left the reserve. No real bird-watcher would have made this mistake. Harrison was therefore a phoney.

3 McCann became suspicious of the telescope bag when Harrison explained that spoonbill were too far away to see with his binoculars. A real bird-watcher would have used his telescope, as Bob and McCann did. It was at this point that McCann wondered if Harrison really had a telescope in his bag.

4 As McCann said, the Tower is the best place to watch the birds at the reserve. And since he was pretending to be a keen bird-watcher, Harrison had to say he had been there. But he said he had used the Tower to watch birds in the Trench – and as Bob and McCann knew, you cannot see the Trench from the Tower.

5 Harrison claimed to have pied kingfishers in his back garden. But as Bob said, this was impossible. Any bird-watcher would know that.

6 Harrison said he did not smoke. So why did he have a box of matches, which he used to light the warden's cigarette?

Useful information

Ham House
Ham Street, Ham, Richmond, Surrey
Tel. 01 940 1950

Young Ornithologists Club
The Lodge, Sandy, Beds
Tel. 0767 80551

Sri Lanka Tourist Board
52 High Holborn, London WC1 6RL
Tel. 405 1194

Watch
22 The Green, Nettleham, Lincoln LN2 2NR
Annual subscription: £2.00 a year or £3.00 for up to 4 members in one family under 18

British Origami Society
193 Abbey Road, Smethwick, Warley, West Midlands
Tel. 021 429 2059

RAF Falcons
No. 1 Parachute Training School
RAF Brize Norton, Nr Carteron, Oxon.
Tel. 0993 842551

Free Admission for Blue Peter Badge Winners
There are now over 20 major Exhibitions and Stately Homes throughout the British Isles that offer free admission to Blue Peter badge winners – provided you take your badge with you! Write to the Blue Peter Office for full details – a stamped, addressed envelope would be appreciated.

Acknowledgements

Co-ordinator: **Gillian Farnsworth**

Designed by **Norman Brownsword** assisted by **Simon Ray-Hills**

Wonder Dog Judy was written by **Dorothy Smith** and illustrated by **Robert Broomfield**

Monster Masks & Claws and *Ear Muffs* by **Margaret Parnell**

The Case of the Twitcher's Telescope was written by **Simon Barnes** and illustrated by **Cindy Lee Wright**

Illustrations in *The Long Drag* were by **Robert Broomfield**; The illustrations from *Where the Wild Things Are* by

Maurice Sendak pp 14–15 are reproduced by permission of the Bodley Head; other illustrations by Selwyn Hutchinson, Richard Geiger, and John Gilkes

Bird photographs pp 44–45 were taken by Eric Hosking; Judy photographs p 54 and 58 reproduced from *The Judy Story – The Dog with Six Lives* by E. Varley, pub. Souvenir Press Ltd; Wild Things, pp 14–16 by permission of Glyndebourne Festival Theatre; all other photographs by David Clarke, Joan Williams, Robert Hill, Barry Boxall, Alex Leger, Michael Turner, Tim Pettigrew, Richard Stanley, and Maureen Blaxland.

BLUE PETER COMPETITION

Would you like to come to TV Centre and meet Simon, Peter and Janet, and Jack and Goldie? This could be your chance to come to London and meet them all at a special party – and see the Blue Peter studio!

CALCULATE THE CABLES

Jennifer James

David McCamley

"WHERE HAS THAT CAT GONE?"

The cartoons of our studio at the back and front of the book were drawn by Blue Peter viewers Jennifer James and David McCamley. They include lots of the cables that help to get the pictures from the cameras and the sounds from the microphones on to the TV screen in your home. There are cables connecting all the studio lights, too. We've asked the BBC's Controller, Resource Operations, TV, Charles Paton, to estimate how many metres of cable there are in the Blue Peter studio.

24 people who give the correct answer will be invited to our

BLUE PETER PARTY ★★

and there'll be lots of competition badges for the runners-up, too!

When you've finished your cable calculating, write your answer on the entry form and send it to:

★ ☆
       Blue Peter
★   **Calculate the Cables**
       Competition
★ ☆ **BBC TV Centre**
       London W12 7RJ

First Prize Winners and runners-up will be notified by letter. The closing date for entries is 11 January, 1985.

There are _____ metres of cable in the Blue Peter studio.

Name _____

Address _____

Age _____

"WHERE HAS T

This cartoon was drawn by 16-year-old David McCamley